Papa's War

From the London Blitz to the Liberation of Holland

Papa's War

From the London Blitz to the Liberation of Holland

To Janet,

I hope you enjoy this book.

Thérèse van Houten

Thérèse van Houten

ISBN: 0692371133
ISBN 13: 9780692371138
Library of Congress Control Number: 2015901011
Cheyne Institute, Washington, DC

*What's past is prologue**
I dedicate this book to my grandchildren, the future:
  Knelis
  Johanna
  Emma
  Madden Marie
  Russell
  Austin
  Tatum
  Eileen
  Jackson
  Sean
  Julian
  Giles

---

* William Shakespeare. *The Tempest*. Act II, scene 1.

TABLE OF CONTENTS

PROLOGUE

Mid-September 1944, Captain Jan van Houten travels from London, England, to Brussels, Belgium, a town that only days ago was liberated from the Germans. Jan's task is to set up a press censorship office in The Netherlands, as soon as this country, too, is free from German occupation. He is sent on this mission by the Dutch government, which since May 1940 has been in exile in London.

The assumption is that within weeks—if not days—the Allied forces will cross the borders from Belgium into The Netherlands and successfully rout the Germans. Little does Jan—or anyone else, for that matter—realize that the liberation of The Netherlands will be a long, drawn-out process. The western provinces, cut off from food supplies, will suffer through the devastating *Honger Winter* until they are freed in May 1945. Jan's goodbye to his wife, Marie, and their three small children is filled with hope: the war will soon be over, within months he will be home again—home then being the lovely Thames-side village of Wraysbury. In fact, except for Jan's infrequent and short visits to England, not until early spring

1947 will Jan and Marie share a home together, this time in The Hague.

During this unexpectedly long separation, Jan and Marie write each other daily, carefully numbering each letter to counteract the vagaries of wartime postal service. To Jan and Marie the letters become a daily ritual, an evening chat describing the day's highs and lows and affirming their love for and commitment to each other. These chats are a continuation of the letters they wrote each other earlier in the war—first in September 1939, when Marie and their infant daughter were evacuated from London, and again a year later during the nine-month bombing of London. Most of the letters have been preserved, as have several diaries.

Papa's War is based primarily on Jan's letters. Historical background and occasionally letters from Marie explain the context in which the letters are written. Jan's early letters include a day-to-day account of life in London during the Blitz and offer an insider's perspective of, and reaction to, the challenges faced by the Dutch government-in-exile. The letters document the development of the wartime Dutch press service and the post-war press censorship and Jan's parallel and unexpected career path. They reflect the ongoing balancing act between press censorship and propaganda—as understood and practiced at the end of World War II by British, Dutch, and American military authorities.

Jan's post-war letters from The Netherlands provide a first-hand account of the hardships civilians endure even after liberation. Jan and his military and press colleagues are eyewitnesses to historic events such as the allied forces' failed attempt to capture a vital bridge over the Rhine at Arnhem—a defeat that delayed the liberation of most Dutch provinces by another eight months; the Queen's visit to the liberated southern provinces; and the long-awaited May 1945 German capitulation.

On a more personal note, Jan's letters record his loneliness during the long months of separation from Marie and the children and his worries about the plight of his parents and siblings in the still-occupied Dutch provinces.

While Jan is Dutch, Marie is the London-born daughter of French parents. As a correspondent for the *Maasbode,* a Dutch newspaper, Jan has been living and working in London since 1931. This is where he first meets Marie, where they are married in September 1937, and where their first child is born in May 1939.

Jan and Marie's joint language is English—with few exceptions, the letters are written in English. A glossary translates the occasional Dutch or French expression—mostly terms of endearment. Two family trees show who's who in Jan's and Marie's families. And then there are photos: the "snaps" of his children that Jan carries with him at all times and proudly displays in his office and billet, and the occasional photos of Jan and his colleagues. There is also a photo of Jan in uniform, the photo that we children kissed each night before going to sleep—for this is the story of my father.

CHAPTER I

ENGLAND AT WAR
September 1939 to September 1940

Jan and Marie's letters and diaries start in August 1939, when Europe is on the brink of war. A year earlier, the Germans had invaded Austria, and in March of 1939 they invaded Czechoslovakia. In response, British Prime Minister Neville Chamberlain, who until then had advocated a policy of appeasement, announces that Britain will resist further German action "to the utmost of its power."[1] By August 1939, Germany is threatening to invade Poland. The possibility of war, however, is not foremost on Jan and Marie's minds as they travel from their home in London, England, to Rotterdam, The Netherlands.* After all, The Netherlands remained neutral during the last world war.

---

* The names "Holland" and "The Netherlands" are often used interchangeably, even though they aren't quite the same. The Netherlands is the name of the entire country. In general conversation, the term Holland is often used when referring to the entire country. In fact, Jan frequently does so in his letters. However, in its narrowest sense, "Holland" refers to two provinces: North Holland and South Holland. These two provinces are home to the country's largest cities: Rotterdam, a major seaport; Amsterdam, the capital; and The Hague, the seat of government.

The purpose of their trip is to visit Jan's family and introduce three-month-old "Treesje"—the Dutch diminutive for Thérèse. But, as Marie writes in her diary, the holiday is soon marred by talk of war.

> **August 24, 1939 [Marie's diary].** Beautiful weather. Getting really sun-tanned! Too much war talk for holiday atmosphere. Sudden appearance of military life everywhere. Think that holiday will soon be over.

Their holiday is indeed cut short when, on August 25, Great Britain and Poland sign a formal treaty of mutual assistance in the event of an attack by Germany.[2] Jan and Marie return to England that same night.

> **August 25 [Marie's diary].** Decide to return to England to avoid rush because of baby. Boat crowded. 1000 on board, beating last night's record of 700. Majority of people German-speaking Jews.

England Declares War
Returning to their apartment on Kings Avenue in southwest London, Marie notes in her dairy that London is "heavily sandbagged, with nothing but lorries of sand passing by." Many of their friends, especially those with small children, are leaving London.

> **August 30 [Marie's diary].** Phoned K. They are leaving London on Monday. C. and children are leaving at weekend. Begin to feel rather deserted.

Marie with Treesje. London. Summer 1939.

T. phoned to say goodbye. She is off to Wales with children. Mrs. V. came in during the morning to tell me that her children were being evacuated tomorrow. Surely there is not going to be a war! The wireless announcer keeps on repeating that the evacuation is only a precaution. It all seems such a horrible dream. Read notice at the school: Schoolchildren to be at school at 7 in the morning. Mothers and children under five to be at school at 1:30 on Saturday. What shall I do? Surely it isn't true that our home must be broken up.

On Friday, September 1, 1939, Germany invades Poland.[3] Jan and Marie decide it is best if Marie and Treesje do indeed leave London. The next morning, with the baby in a travel basket, Marie goes to the evacuation site having no idea what her final destination will be.

September 2 [Marie's diary]. Felt very muddle-headed. It all seemed so impossible. Packed a case with baby's things and one with mine to be sent on later. Packed Treesje's travel cradle with as many napkins and covers as would fit under mattress without tipping Treesje out! Strapped her in for safety. Arrived at school armed with baby in basket and hatbox, as this could go over my arm. Caught train at 4:10. Not knowing where we were going, we were surprised and delighted to find ourselves taken to the south coast, to Shoreham. Here we were greeted by nurses, Girl

Jan and Marie's first home.
Avenue House, King's Avenue, SW London.

Guides, and many helpers. Given cups of tea and a bag of rations each to last 24 hours. Driven by coach to village eight miles inland. Here found billeting officer, helpers, fleets of private cars, and lemonade and biscuits! Driven to billet in Henfield, Sussex. I am with old lady of 82 and her companion. Everyone so very kind. Shown to bedroom lit by two candles, but spotlessly clean.

The next day, September 3, England declares war on Germany.[4] Marie reports that the declaration of war was immediately followed by a siren.

September 3 [Marie's diary]. For some unknown reason thought I was to be killed at any moment! Tried on my gas mask for the first time—horrible smelly thing. Kept two wet napkins with me to put over Treesje's face should there be gas, as we have not our baby [gas] bags yet. After ¾ hr, life as usual. Everyone wondering whether alarm was rehearsal or real.

In London, Jan writes his first of many letters to Marie—on this day that happens to be their second wedding anniversary.

> **September 3 [Letter from Jan to Marie].** I had promised you a holiday in September, at a place where you could take Treesje. But not like this. All my hopes were shattered this morning when I listened in to the fateful announcement. Now we are at war with Germany. And to make things even more real, the first air raid warning was sounded. The only thing I could say was "Thank God, Marie and the little one are away." Your wire put my mind fully at ease. I have not been able to find out where exactly you are, but as the telegram came from Brighton you should not be far from the sea.

Jan continues his work in the London office of the *Maasbode* where things aren't quite what they used to be. A major difference for Jan is the involvement of the British censors in the transmission of copy to The Netherlands. After writing his articles at his Fleet Street office, he must travel to the British Ministry of Information to have his copies approved by the censors. Only then may the copy be transmitted by phone to The Netherlands. To Marie, he writes:

---

* Unless otherwise indicated, all subsequent entries are letters, or excerpts from letters, from Jan to Marie.

September 20. Did all my work at the office, in Dutch. Went to the Ministry and found that all the calls had been booked beforehand and that they could not let me speak until after midnight. I nearly fainted. On top of that I was told that there was no Dutch-speaking censor available, so that if I wanted to get anything through, I had to translate the whole bally lot. Did I kick up a row! I went with my difficulties higher up and managed to get a promise that they were willing to try to get my call through at 10, if I translated my stuff. I did so, and at 10:15 passed all my news to Holland. Holland will never have realized what a damn lot of work that meant to me. I then groped my way home in the pitch dark.

Jan's press pass for the Dutch daily, *De Maasbode*.
London. January 1940.

The mandatory blackout is designed to make it difficult for German bombers to find their target. It not only means blackout curtains at all windows, but also no streetlights for the duration of the war.

Preparing for a Possible Invasion

The British sometimes refer to the period from September 1939 until May 1940 as the "phoney" war.[5] Britain is at war, but nothing much is happening yet. On October 28, Marie and Treesje return from Henfield to London, where preparations are underway for a possible attack by the Germans. Jan and Marie get used to food rationing, which starts in January 1940 under the newly established Ministry of Food. Before the war, the English produced less than 40 percent of their food supply. Foreseeing that the Germans might attack shipping bound for the United Kingdom with the intent of cutting off food supplies, the government rations what food is available and increases food production within the country.

Marie and Jan receive a ration book containing coupons for two adults and one infant. At first only bacon, butter, and sugar are rationed. These are followed by meat, tea, jam, biscuits, breakfast cereals, cheese, eggs, milk, and canned fruit. Other rationed items include clothing, textiles, soap, and coal. Bread is one of the few foods not rationed during the war.[6]

Gas masks are issued to children and adults. There is an attempt to make the children's gas masks less scary by having them look like cartoon characters. Special masks are issued to babies. The masks are issued because during World War I, the Germans had introduced gas warfare.[7] As it turns out, the masks are never needed. Yet throughout the war, English children walk to school carrying their masks in little brown cardboard boxes with a string handle.

As Jan and Marie live in an apartment, their planning does not include building an Anderson or other type of air raid shelter. The designated safe place in their building is the hallway of one of the ground-level flats. Marie's mother and younger sister Agnes, who live in a single-family house in the Clapham area of London, do build a shelter in their garden. These shelters are small hut-like structures sunk three feet into the ground with the tops and sides covered in earth. They prove to be extremely effective against anything less than a direct hit. The government distributes more than two million of them before the bombing begins in September 1940.[8] Until then, however, Jan and Marie cannot envision the many nights over a nine-month period that Jan will sleep in such a shelter.

Capitulation of The Netherlands

In the early morning hours of May 10, 1940, the German *Wehrmacht* invades The Netherlands—a swift airborne attack that takes the country by surprise. Dutch armed forces succeed at some initial resistance—slowing the German advance and preventing the planned capture of the royal family at The Hague. On May 12, following this foiled attempt, the queen's daughter, Princess Juliana leaves for England with her husband, Prince Bernard and their two small daughters, Beatrix and Irene.[9]

However, it is clear that the Dutch armed forces can only slow down, but not counter, the invaders. Therefore, on the day of the invasion, the Dutch Minister of Foreign Affairs, Eelco van

Kleffens, and the Minister of Colonies, Charles Welter, travel to England to request military support from the British. Their sudden departure is not without danger. One of the two seaplanes waiting in Scheveningen (a fishing village outside The Hague) is shot down within minutes of lifting off. Its occupants, three young sailors, are killed. In a book describing the first year of the war, *Juggernaut over Holland*, Van Kleffens reports that the flight is so last minute that there is no map on board. Because of a fuel leak, the plane in which he travels lands at the nearest English beach—Brighton. To signal their peaceful intentions, the plane's wireless operator climbs onto one of the wings, waving a white handkerchief.[10]

On the third day of the invasion, May 13, Queen Wilhelmina escapes to London on a British destroyer to avoid capture by the Germans and to ensure that there will still be a government—even if it means a government-in-exile.** Queen Wilhelmina is met in London by King George VI.[11] Her first radio proclamation to The Netherlands is sent from Buckingham Palace. Announcing that the government is now located in England, she explains: "In this way the territory of The Netherlands, whether in Europe, the East or West Indies, remains one sovereign state, whose voice as a full-fledged member of our allies can continue to be heard."[12]

The Dutch army's valiant defense is shattered when Hitler decides that the most efficient way to conquer Holland is to destroy its

_____

** Queen Wilhelmina resigns from the throne in 1948 in favor of her daughter Juliana, who reigns until 1980. Juliana's daughter Beatrix reigns from 1980 to 2013. The current monarch is Beatrix's son, King Willem Alexander. Source: "Members of the Royal House." www.koninklijkhuis.nl .

major cities, starting with Rotterdam. The bombing of Rotterdam on May 14, 1940, is as devastating as it is unexpected.[13] One square mile of the city is leveled. More than 800 residents are killed and 80,000 are made homeless.

The destruction of Rotterdam and Germany's threat to bomb other Dutch cities forces The Netherlands to surrender on May 15. 1940. For the next five years, until its liberation in May 1945, the country is under the civil administration of Arthur Seyss-Inquart, an Austrian Nazi appointed by Hitler to be the *Reichskommissar* of the occupied Netherlands territories.[14]

The Exiled Dutch Government

The Dutch capitulation results in the immediate evacuation of Dutch cabinet ministers to London on May 14. Their sudden departure from their offices means that most arrive without their wives or children, let alone staff.[15]

A key member of the new government-in-exile, Adriaan Pelt, travels to London from Geneva that same day. Well before the war, Minister Van Kleffens had realized that if Holland were to be attacked, the country would need a Dutch press service to present the country's needs and interests to the world and to counteract German propaganda. Pelt, then in charge of the information service of the League of Nations, is the person whom Van Kleffens judges is best suited for this task.[16] Jan, along with other Dutch journalists who happen to be working in London at that time, is recruited by Pelt to help set up this new press office within the exiled Dutch government.

Views of the bomb damage in Rotterdam. May 1940.
Photos taken within days of the bombing by Jan's brother, Martien van Houten.

One of the last government experts to leave the country is Ton Speekenbrink, then a functionary in the Ministry of Commerce, Industry, and Shipping. On the morning of May 15, 1940—the day of the Dutch capitulation—he is told by the Dutch Secretary General to join the Dutch legation in London. With wife and four small children, he finds passage that evening on the very last ship leaving Holland, the *Texelstroom*, carrying German prisoners of war. Despite damage caused by German fire, the ship arrives safely in Dover.[17]

Leading Dutch industrialists and businessmen living in London at the time offer immediate assistance to the newly arriving Cabinet. It is thanks to Royal Dutch Shell that within weeks the government is able to rent four floors at Stratton House on Piccadilly. Shell and Unilever are among the companies that assist with administrative personnel and other resources. The Dutch department store C&A

on Oxford Street provides a bomb shelter as well as office space. At one point, the office of Prince Bernard is on the building's top floor.[18]

The Dutch Colony in London

At the outbreak of the war, some 6,000 Dutch are living in England, including journalists like Jan, industrialists, and representatives of a range of Dutch companies. In the first few weeks after the invasion, an additional 1,600 Dutch civilians arrive in England.[19] Many of those who manage to escape in the first days after the invasion are writers, social critics, and politicians who know that they are likely German targets. They include Dutch Jewish intellectuals and writers who in Holland have been outspoken critics of Germany. Several become part of the Dutch media apparatus in London, including Meijer Sluijser, the author of a series of articles on the plight of Jews in Eastern Europe, and Marcus van Blankenstein, journalist and vocal critic of National Socialism (Nazi-ism).

Foremost among this group of refugees is Louis de Jong, historian and journalist, who escapes with his wife by ship to England immediately after The Netherlands capitulates. On the day of his departure, at the port of Ijmuiden, near Amsterdam, he is separated from his parents and twin brother. He never sees them again.[20]After the war, De Jong becomes the director of the *Rijksinstituut voor Oorlogsdocumentatie* (The Netherlands' State Institute for War Documentation). He is the author of a 14-volume history of The Netherlands during World War II.

This initial wave of refugees is later joined by some 1,800 so-called *Engelandvaarders*.[21] These "England-farers" derive their name from the few (about 150) who manage to make it across the North Sea by sailboat or even canoe. Such travel by sea soon becomes increasingly difficult, if not impossible, when in 1942, the Germans build a coastal defense, known as the Atlantic Wall, to prevent attacks from England as well as escapes by sea. This wall (not in fact a wall, but a series of bunkers, mined beaches, and other fortifications) eventually stretches from Norway to Spain.[22]

The majority of *Engelandvaarders* therefore arrive in England not by boat, but through a hazardous overland journey through Belgium, France, and Spain to neutral Portugal or, less frequently, to Gibraltar. Others are able to make it to neutral Sweden. From these nations, lucky refugees are able to get a flight to England.

A number of Engelandvaarders are recruited into Pelt's Press Office. Mentioned here are several who become good friends of Jan and Marie. Jan de Hartog is a Dutch author whose novel about Dutch seamen, *Hollands Glorie*, happens to be published shortly before the invasion. Although apolitical, this tale of Dutch sailors battling the sea becomes a symbol of Dutch courage and resistance. The Gestapo's resulting interest in De Hartog forces him to flee to London. Herman de Man, a convert from Judaism to Catholicism is living in France at the outbreak of the war—separated from his Dutch wife and seven children. He manages to make his way to England but is unable to help his family flee Holland. After the war he learns that his wife and all but two of his children have been deported. Henk van den Broek, a Paris-based Dutch journalist, joins the exodus from Paris after the French capitulation in June 1940, and makes it to London via Portugal.

Queen Wilhelmina has great respect and admiration for the *Engelandvaarders*. Throughout the war, she invites these new arrivals, regardless of their background—at first individually, and later in groups—to tea. To her, they are a source of inspiration as well as a means of learning what is happening in The Netherlands.[23]

The Battle of Britain

The conquest of not only Holland, but of Belgium and France as well (in May and June 1940), brings Germany closer to Hitler's planned invasion of England. To overcome the last barrier, the North Sea, the German *Luftwaffe* launches a major air offensive on British air and sea defenses. The aim of this offensive is to weaken the British Royal Air Force (RAF) so that it won't stand in the way of the German fleet when it attacks England. The Battle of Britain lasts from July to October 1940. With the help of its radar, the RAF wins. For now, Germany has to cancel plans to invade Britain.[24]

Referring to the RAF's success at holding off a German invasion, Winston Churchill—who, in May 1940, has succeeded Chamberlain as Prime Minister of Britain[25]—utters these well-known words: "Never in the field of human conflict was so much owed by so many to so few."

During the final phases of the Battle of Britain, the German *Luftwaffe* conducts nightly raids of Britain's airfields. In September, the *Luftwaffe* switches to daytime raids of airfields and nightly bombing raids on London. This is the beginning of the Blitz, short for the German term *Blitzkrieg*, meaning "lightning war."[26]

CHAPTER II

THE LONDON BLITZ
September 1940 to May 1941

The Germans bomb London almost nightly from September 1940 to May 1941. Despite the RAF's efforts to intercept the bombs, by the end of September the Blitz has killed 6,954 civilians.[27] During the first few months, the bombing goes on for 57 days in a row. One in six Londoners becomes homeless.

Evacuation from London

Jan and Marie don't know whether they, too, are counted among the homeless, but the Blitz does indeed result in the loss of their home. During the first few weeks of September, Jan, Marie, and Treesje (now 16 months old) sleep every night on the hall floor of downstairs neighbors. Marie's daytime routine is interspersed with dashes to the nearest shelter in response to sirens warning of an imminent air raid.

However, on Saturday, September 14, following a night of heavy bombing in their neighborhood, Marie has no choice but once again to leave London—this time it will be for ten long months.

Close friends, Eileen and Frank Keegan, have been urging her to come and stay with them and their three young children—Clare, John, and Anthony—in Taunton, Somerset. The Keegans have moved to Taunton because Frank, a school inspector, has been placed in charge of the evacuated London schoolchildren who are billeted with host families in Somerset and the adjoining areas of Wiltshire and Dorset.[28] Frank and Eileen are especially concerned about Marie and Treesje, knowing that at this point Marie is nearly seven months pregnant. Jan's letter, written the day after her departure, confirms that Marie made the right choice.

> **September 15, 1940.** I don't know where to start. So many questions to ask, how you got on, how Treesje behaved, how you found the Keegans, whether you have had raids or not, etc. etc. Everything has gone so quickly that I can hardly realize that you have gone away. What that is going to mean for me, you know only too well, but you know too that it is a great relief to me, that you two are now in safer regions, and that you can have rest again. Don't think that I exaggerate, but there is not a great deal left of Clapham Park Road. We heard Mass in St. Mary's Hall, which had not a piece of glass whole. We could only get there by walking in the centre of the road, as a great number of houses are on the point of tumbling over. The whole district around there has been evacuated. It is a real devastated area.
>
> **September 16.** Thank all guardian angels in heaven for having escaped the greatest, ghastliest, and most terrifying experiences ever. Kings Avenue has been

bombed. I am alive and kicking, so are the rest of the people in the flats. All our windows are intact but we are just about the only place in the whole neighborhood which has not suffered, apart from some cracks in the walls. Opposite us not a window is whole. The sight is ghastly.

Our roof received a number of hits of incendiary bombs, which lay burning in the street in front of the house.* At the back of the house, the smoke was even thicker and we could not see half way down the road.

The damage round Clapham North [station] and Clapham Road was continued during the most terrible night we have ever had. We stayed up until the all-clear this morning. Smelling burning, [a neighbour] and I went up to see if the roof had caught it. Upstairs we saw three huge fires around the Common Way. A "whistler" threw us down for a few minutes and we thought the flat was hit, but miraculously we escaped again. The garage next to the Ks' burned out. Clapham Court Mansions received a number of small hits. Queens Court and the fire station in Kings Avenue got a high explosive. The timber yard near Clapham North station went up in flames. One block of those old stately homes was

---

* If these incendiary bombs do not catch fire immediately they can be dowsed by sand. At first the British set up organization of volunteer firewatchers trained to dowse these bombs before the fire spread. Later, fire-watching duties become compulsory. Source: Edwin Webb and John Duncan, *Blitz over Britain* (Turnbridge Wells: Spellmont, Ltd, 1990), 42.

reduced to splinters. Not a window in Bedford Road and side streets is intact. I hope that the above gives you reason to be grateful that you have left the place.

Pelt offered me to come and stay with him. Address your letters therefore to the office where I'll get them for certain. Another siren has gone and the guns are blasting away. *Dag lieve kindje.* Don't worry. I will be all right. Let us pray for one another. All my love and *une bise* for Treesje.

Jan's new position with the Dutch Information Service requires him to remain in London. To escape the nightly bombing, he accepts an offer to stay with friends, Jan and Toos Hazebroek, in Ealing, a western suburb of London. The Hazebroeks have a small concrete shelter in the garden. Their two young children, Marion and Ernst, sleep in bunks while the parents sleep on a mattress on the floor.

September 18. Very pleased and relieved to learn that you are enjoying so much peace. I am now writing from Jan Hazebroek's dining room. Tuesday night, I had to leave the office during a raid—they never stop nowadays—and took a train to Ealing after having phoned Jan that I might be coming. They retire to their shelter every night at 8, or earlier if the raid starts before. The first night I sat in their shelter until 9:30 talking, or rather, whispering so as not to awaken the kids. Then went to bed in the hall where my bed is put up for permanent use. Very comfortable indeed. Slept like a log. Some very

distant gunfire scares them here, but it is nothing
for people with Clapham experience!

He vividly describes "life as usual" in a city hit nightly by heavy
bombing.

> **September 21.** The sights in the subways are appall-
> ing. At 5 in the evening, people are stretched out
> already for the night. All along the line, mothers
> with their kids, whole families seeking safety put-
> ting up with unbelievable discomfort. Civilization
> 1940! My God, are we all mad!

Marie's letters to Jan reassure him that she and Treesje are well and
are fully settled in their new home, where Eileen has given Marie
and Treesje the bedroom of their youngest son.

> **September 20 [Letter from Marie to Jan].** Taunton
> is packed with evacuees and refugees. Many people
> from Hastings who have been turned out of their
> homes are billeted here. It's unbelievable not to hear
> sirens and to be able to go for walks in the park with
> no second thought as to when the siren will go.*

She is quite matter-of-fact about the occasional Taunton air raid.
Most are for the nearby Bristol airport.[29]

---

* Because of the German bombing and the possibility of a German landing in the area
many residents are evacuated from Hastings. By September 1940, the town's population, formerly 66,000, is down to 22,000. Victoria Seymour. "Hastings in WWII."
www.victoriaseymour.com

September 27 [Letter from Marie to Jan]. I had just finished my shopping when a siren sounded! I had almost forgotten what one sounded like. Even Treesje didn't put her arms out to be picked up! A butcher nearby told me to come in. He helped me bring the pram in and unstrap Treesje, and was most anxious that she should not be frightened. He then helped me down to the cellar. We were about eight or nine people down there, and Treesje showed off for all she was worth! This is the third siren Taunton has had since the war was declared and they have never been more serious than this morning's although once one did last for five hours.

Jan's Life during the Blitz

Reassured that Marie and Treesje are well, Jan adjusts to nights in the relative safety of Ealing and a long commute to his office in central London—a commute that is all too often delayed by bomb damage.

September 24. Most people are now carrying a tin hat about with them. It is sometimes necessary as shrapnel is flying all over the shop when there's a raid on. These hats are expensive and not so easy to get. The guns are booming away just now. Ealing had one hit last night, but far enough away not to feel the shock. I took shelter under the stairs.

Round the station, one or two hits were scored, and it took me 1½ hours to get to London since the signals of both railway lines had been smashed up. I wonder what it is going to be like when the early darkness sets in. It might be suicidal to go home. I am angling for shelter under C&A, where some ministers are spending the night too.

As much as Jan appreciates the safety of the Hazebroek's shelter, he dreads the nights he has to spend there. There really isn't room for an additional adult.

September 26. Jan and Toos have put a mattress in their shelter for me. Awfully good of them, as it cramps us all. It is a bit awkward too, having a foreign body present since [chamber] pots might have to be used. Still we are at war!

September 30. Our flat is still standing but without any windows. The flying glass does not seem to have done any damage to the furniture.

October 1. Many windows down this way have been broken through blast and shrapnel, large pieces of which we collect in the morning in the garden.

October 8. A tremendous explosion nearly threw me off my chair. I was waiting for the roof to come down, ready to hide under the table, but nothing further happened. That's why I could not finish my letter last night. After the great shock, I waited a moment and then rushed to the shelter. Even the concrete shelter had swayed! We listened to the shrapnel clattering against the house and discussed the terrible dampness of the shelter after Sunday's rain. I really did not want to sleep there, but I felt it wiser in view of the constant activity overhead.

October 9. Hate going to the shelter. It is so damp that if you leave your matches there for one night they will not light. I have no sheet or anything damp-proof under my little mattress.

One of Jan's letters, although humorous in tone, reveals some of the stresses of these living arrangements.

October 11. Dear Madam, I have great pleasure in sending you the timetable of events since my interrupted descriptions of last night. Went pyjama-less to shelter (dressing gown though) and was informed that since my only pair, which I had worn since the beginning of serious hostilities—mind you in the air—had started to smell, it was dispatched to a laundry nearby, which still stands, and that I had to take one of Mr. H. from his dresser. And a well-fitted one it was. I liked the one which I chose. Nice and warm. Toos nearly woke the kids—the greatest crime in our shelter life—when she observed that I had picked Jan's newest and most expensive flannel one, especially reserved for very special occasions. Although I could not quite see what special occasions have to do with the colour and warmth of pyjamas, I felt very guilty and promised Jan that he would be allowed to wear one of my new woollen ones. It did not seem to quite pacify Toos. Slept well till 7, when I had to get up from my hall bed, in view of the new nanny who might not be able to resist the sight of a man in such beautiful pyjamas in bed.

However, on more than once occasion Jan mentions that his hosts enjoy having another adult with them to relieve the nightly tedium of being cooped up in a small, damp shelter. A favorite pastime is playing word games.

Jan faces daily difficulties getting to and from work. The relentless air raids bring about an ever-changing obstacle course: streets destroyed by bombs; streets blocked by time bombs; and stations, rail lines, and signals destroyed.

October 12. It was a most beastly morning with raids and traffic delays. I arrived at the office dead beat, having travelled by about five means of transport to get near my office. This afternoon going home was even worse. They are trying to take away the time bomb outside the Ritz.*

---

* Unexploded delayed action time bombs present a major hazard. By the end of October 1940, in London alone, 3,000 unexploded bombs are waiting to be disposed of. Source: Edwin Webb and John Duncan, op. cit., 43.

October 14. You will be interested and probably relieved to know that steps have been taken to reduce the dampness of our shelter. I have a sheet. My mattress and covers are all aired during the day in the kitchen and for many hours a day a fire is being burned in the shelter. It was necessary since the kids are already suffering from colds.

October 15. I slept like a log last night despite London's most terrible assault. Having dinner during a terrific barrage by our guns certainly was no treat, but when I heard a jerry dive that sounded to me right over our place, I thought it wiser to join the family. Protected by blanket and a frying pan (as helmet), I rushed from the home to the shelter and had just time to watch the most amazing sight. Three huge flares were hanging, not more than a hundred yards away, probably over the railroad junction. I could see the threads and the slowly descending lights, which lit the district like daylight. Hardly back in the safety of the shelter, where Jan looked pale like this paper, three long whistlers came down. The place rocked but to my amazement the house had withstood the blast.

The stories everyone has to tell are staggering. Went to see De Man's flat. What an escape. Two hits on two of these small flats, and they got away with shock only. We had to climb over the debris to get there. Bogaert had slept at the Ministry and found upon going home (a large flat near Paddington) that everything was gone. The suit he is wearing is all that is left of all his possessions. The picture of his mother can be seen from the street—hanging on a partly standing wall. Destruction in central London has been wicked. We are closing down at 5 in order to get home before the raids.

By now, Jan and Marie's once lovely flat is boarded up and uninhabitable. For several months, they pay rent and even utility rates so they have a place to store furniture and other belongings. When Marie's mother offers to store things in her front room, they give up the flat. Both look back on it rather wistfully.

October 14 [Letter from Marie to Jan]. I am longing for the day when I can run our own little home again—I hope it will be quite soon. I miss Treesje's high chair and our lovely bedroom and Treesje's cupboard and our beautiful, comfortable dining room. I may say that mayn't I? I'm not grumbling— only daydreaming. I have not any reason to grumble as I am happy and comfortable with Treesje, and my Jan is as comfortable and happy as is possible under these conditions. What a pity that the war ever started.

Jan replies in a similar vein.

> **October 23.** I so well understand: When will the day come that we shall be in our own familiar surroundings again? We have such lovely things! Often do I think of that cosy corner near the [tea] trolley with all my papers around me.

Visits to Taunton

Jan manages a trip to Taunton about every three to four weeks. It is clear that he lives for these brief visits, no matter how tiring the journey, how complicated the logistics, and how crowded the trains. The closer it gets to December 1st—Marie's due date—the more difficult the constant parting becomes for Jan.

> **November 11.** I lay back in my train seat thinking of the little tears, which my *schatje* could not withhold. There were reasons for some sadness. Parting always hurts. This time it got me too a bit. So much had I wanted to stay near my *vrouwtje*, to be with her in those last few days.
>
> I ended up in a compartment where there was room only for two people. I was closely hugged in between the window and a very fleshy hip. The first effort of getting into my pocket cost me a tear in my raincoat, which had got caught against a sharp point of an ashtray. Very annoyed, of course. The women just kept on looking as

sheepish as ever, and did not dream of pulling in a bit. As those two kept on eating things out of a great variety of bags and boxes, I felt that I would be even more squeezed as time went on, and took my refuge in the buffet car. A comfortable seat, a coffee, and a quite early snack-lunch brought a pleasant *intermezzo* in an otherwise rather dull journey. Waiting people forced me to give up my comfort!

The November 11 visit to Taunton is Jan's last one before the baby's birth.

November 14. *Vrouwtje* sounds so cheerful and happy that I got into a cheery mood too and in the strength of it ordered 50 cigars. I shall smoke fewer cigarettes and hope to have sufficient left, when the new baby arrives, to treat my colleagues.

The ongoing bombing has become so routine that Jan's letters now mention only unusual events. For instance, in mid-November, he describes the removal of a large unexploded time bomb near his office.

November 18. At half past two a warning was given that we should go to the shelter as a dangerous time bomb would pass our building. Nearly all took the tip, nearly all found a good place to watch a lorry go by with a bomb so big that I cannot possibly imagine how such a thing could ever be transported by a plane. Still there it is. And then I read in the paper that those heroes who remove these objects don't get any extra pay. All in a day's work!

December 2. *Mijn lieveling,* I feel just as I did before our marriage. Full of love and full of happy expectation. May be that this letter has to be forwarded to you in the nursing home or may be that it finds you at Eileen's still quietly waiting for things to happen.* In the latter case let it be to you as additional encouragement, that I am so full of love for you at the moment that I have been trying hard for a means to express it other than by just some poor words. *Kindje.* I am bubbling over with love for you. Do you hear that? I wish I could whisper it into your ears. Your Jan, almost a daddy of two little ones.

Marie Colette is born on December 4. Jan arrives the next day to meet his new baby daughter. Although Marie won't be allowed out of bed until eight days later, Jan may take little Colette—a mere three days old—to the local church to be baptized. At the time, baptism within days after birth is a common practice among Catholics. Colette's godparents are the two friends who have taken in the homeless family, Jan Hazebroek and Eileen Keegan. Jan returns to London on December 8, wishing he could have stayed longer.

---

* Marie's planning for the baby has included deciding whether to have the baby in a hospital or a nursing home. Both settings will provide a two-week in-patient stay following childbirth, as is the norm at the time. Marie choses the nursing home and is delighted to learn that a private room is available.

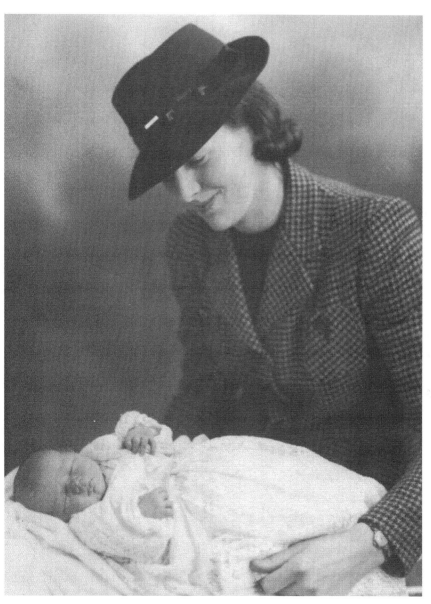

Colette and her godmother, Eileen Keegan
Taunton. December 7, 1940.

December 9. Where should I begin? I am crammed full of things I want to talk about with my *schatje*, and feel I cannot cope with it all. Some chronological order may help me. Frank saw me off. I left Treesje in the car with John and Clare, and did not even kiss her goodbye. Why? Probably because I felt so highly strung that I might have shown tears. I waited an hour before the train rolled in.

Why should I feel such a tremendous longing for a home, a home of our own? *Vrouwtje* knows the answer. We are in love, in love with one another, in love with our God-given little kids. I so badly want you with me, you with our precious little possessions. Nobody can give Treesje what we can give her. It is the crime of this war, to separate the parents from their children. I saw my *vrouwtje* again, with Treesje, delighted, running round her bed, peeping over her little sister's cot. What a picture to remember. I saw my little Coletje in your arms, at your breast. God is good to us. Should I even grumble, if not all is going as I should want?

Very slowly we drove into Paddington station. The raid was on and how! By tube I went to Ealing. The sight at Nottingham Gate, where the lifts were out of order, and travellers had to try to find their way along the iron round staircase, made me again thank God for our well-off existence. On both sides of the staircase, men, women, and children were lying or sitting, a terrible indictment of what the world has come to. On the platform the sight was even ghastlier. There was hardly room for passengers to stand along the line. Eight in a row, hundreds of people were lying there, with or without blankets, trying to find peace and safety. One little girl startled me. She looked very pale and ill, and was supporting her little head against the stone wall. There was hardly any room for her to stretch out. However much we might have to put up with, through real or supposed little troubles, it is all nothing compared with this intense misery of the London masses.

The walk from the station to home was rather terrifying. Guns flashing lit up the sky and made one feel on a real battlefield. I took shelter for a minute or so at an ARP [Air Raids Precaution] post and then gradually made my way home. The gunfire remained terrific—the sky over London was flaming red, reflecting the many fires raging.

December 12. Many times during the day, my thoughts flow to my *schatje* far away in Somerset, who has given me so much happiness already, to my Treesje, whom I miss more now than I ever realized, to my little Coletje, whom I should so much would like to watch develop in her first few weeks.

The Blitz Continues

Jan is fortunate to miss the December 29 bombing, as he is making an after-Christmas visit to Taunton. On that night, the *Luftwaffe* firebombs kill close to 3,000 civilians. So many incendiary bombs are dropped that they cause 1,500 fires in the City of London.[30] Returning home on New Year's Day, Jan reassures Marie.

> **January 1, 1941.** By the way, the Sunday fire had not touched Ealing. In fact, things have been quiet here.

Compulsory firewatcher training and service in instituted in February 1941.[31] This is in part a result of the huge fires that raged in London as a result of the December 29 raid. Jan now serves on the rotating schedule of nightly Ealing firewatchers.

Jan's volunteer fire-fighting card.
The London borough of Ealing. Issued March 1941.

March 7, 1942. I should have been with you tonight, but instead I am fire watching, of all things!

March 9. Jerry is very noisy. I am going to sleep. It is 9 and I want to have a good rest. I am fire watching from 2 to 4. Hazebroek from 4 till 6. If there is any alert, I have to be about from 2 to 6. It is no sinecure.

From Jan's perspective, one of the worst raids occurs in early April 1941.

April 4. I have escaped the worst Blitz ever, while "peacefully" working on an article. To be very honest, I had to spend an hour in the shelter as there were so many flares and coloured balloons hanging over the district around us that I really feared an attack on Ealing. The sky overhead was dark red. It looked grand in all its terribleness. When I tell you that tonight at 7, when Bogaert and I walked past several of the hit spots, fires were still blasting away, especially at Leicester Square and between Piccadilly and Dudley's shop, you have some idea of what the West End has had to go through.

Many well-known places are but empty shells. They have made a hell of a mess of Piccadilly and poor old Soho! One of the large Peacock tenements at the back of the Shaftsbury Theatre was partly destroyed, a terrible sight, especially when you are told that there were only few bodies recovered. Bogaert has had his dose of war too. A great many soldiers of a nearby hostel were brought into the Ministry of Information, many dead. It has been a night of terror, though I personally have experienced little fear. I knew that *vrouwtje* always prays that I may get through safely, and that her prayers carry weight. I added a few Hail Marys myself last night.

Another Temporary Home

In January 1941, Marie, fully recuperated from the baby's birth, starts looking for a new place to live. Staying at the Keegans with a newborn and a toddler is too much of an imposition. Moreover, Eileen and Frank are expecting their fourth child. The room where Marie and the children are staying will soon be needed for the new baby.

The ongoing bombing means that it isn't safe to look for a place closer to London. Not that Taunton doesn't continue to have an occasional raid. There was even one during Marie's stay in the nursing home with Colette, as Marie told Jan in one of the letters she wrote at that time.

> **December 17 [Letter from Marie to Jan].** Nurse explained to me that under the stairs they have some bales of cotton wool. [During a raid], they placed a mattress over them, and lay Colette and the other babies on there.

After considerable difficulty and many dead ends, Marie finds rooms with a Mr. and Mrs. Williams in Taunton. She and the children move to their new quarters on February 1, 1941.

February 2, 1941 [Letter from Marie to Jan]. Exactly five months ago today I arrived in Taunton and today I arrived in yet another new home. Both babies went to bed very well. Treesje seemed at home directly which was a great relief. Frank drove my suitcases and the cradle round this morning before going to work. Last night we took the cot round on the old pram. When we left this place Frank suggested pushing me so I accepted and he pushed me all the way home in the pram! I got home safely thank you, altho' Frank did try pretty hard to tip the pram.

Mrs. Williams is a good old soul and understands children. She has three sons of 22, 28, and 35.

Spent a most comfortable and warm night. Treesje very good, also Marie Colette, of course. Really good digs.

Jan is quite reassured to know that Marie and the little ones have settled in so nicely.

February 16. You don't know how pleased I was to read that you seem to get on famously in your new home. It is the best solution under the circumstances and I feel grateful that you are able to make the best of things in the way you are doing. If

Treesje is prepared to accept the big change, without being upset, it would be grand. After all, the little mite must miss her playmates.

Jan continues his visits to Taunton whenever possible. A planned visit in early March has to be cancelled because of a last-minute work deadline. Then a few days later he suddenly realizes that he might have missed visiting Marie the week of her birthday.

> **March 10.** A horrible confession I have to make I have forgotten when it's your birthday. Not the 15th March, I hope. It is 15 or 16th April, my memory tells me, but I dare not rely on it. Tho' it is a strange thing to do, I have to ask you, to tell me. Don't be upset about such nonchalance; I don't love you an iota less for all that. Tell me that you know I do, even if you want to tell me off for my forgetting that important day in your and our lives (it may be that I am subconsciously refusing to admit that you grow older).

The Blitz Ends

The Blitz finally ends in May 1941.[32] Jan moves from his temporary quarters in Ealing to the home of Marie's mother in the London district of Clapham. Now starts his difficult search for a home for the family within commuting distance of London.

Until, then Jan continues the daily letter writing.

CHAPTER III

THE DUTCH PRESS SERVICE
May 1940 to May 1941

Though Jan and his colleagues may spend their nights scrambling for safe shelter, their days are taken up with the dissemination of information that will help the plight of occupied Holland. The Dutch press service in London is known as the RPD [*Regeringspersdienst*—the Government Press Service]. Its objective is clear and straightforward: to strengthen the image of Holland through radio, press, and film.[33] Equally important are providing accurate information to the civilian population in occupied Holland and counteracting German propaganda.

Jan's letters to Marie in Taunton indicate that initially roles within the RPD are loosely defined. At first, Pelt assigns Jan to the RPD's news agency. Within six months, however, Jan is transferred from the RPD's news agency to its press service.

Jan's Role as a Press Officer
Jan finds his new assignment as a press officer extremely interesting. In a letter to Marie, he describes his new position as "really a

gem of a job. I am simply delighted in the work which I am allowed to do now." His main responsibility as press officer is to serve as a liaison to British and foreign correspondents—a role he will keep during his time in London. This work includes making sure that information that is published is in fact correct—as illustrated by this anecdote:

> **October 11, 1940.** I learned that the *Daily Express* had scooped a narrow escape by Prince Bernard [an emergency plane landing]. To satisfy all inquiries about the truth of this report—phones out of order—I cabbed to his house, where I found him on the point of leaving. A most congenial and charming personality. Gave me the dope. Which I phoned through from a box, and before I had arrived back the story was out on the tapes.

As press officer, Jan also serves as a link between the RPD and the British press as well as foreign correspondents confirming and providing information for articles on conditions in The Netherlands. He is quite pleased when his initial contact with Prince Bernard results in a contact with a journalist friend of the Prince.

> **October 17.** I felt quite honored when Prince Bernard phoned and asked whether he could send a friend journalist to come and see me to collect some information.

The London tradition of restaurant lunches provides Jan with far more than his one warm meal a day, but also strengthens his contacts with the British and foreign press. He especially enjoys the occasional meal in an exclusive restaurant, often with senior British and Dutch government officials or well-known personalities.

October 23. I had lunch at *L'Escargot* and enjoyed my *apéritif,* my *vin rosé,* and my *grenouilles.** Next time I'll take my *vrouwtje.*

November 16. I have a few more business lunches on my books, one with the city writer of the *Evening Standard* and the money editor of the *Financial News.*

November 18. [Lunched] with a charming chap from the Ministry of Economic Warfare, who had taken me to his club some time ago. *Vrouwtje* must think that her man is not doing too badly. But don't forget, I am really working very hard, and sometimes feel that it is too much. Never mind, I am lots happier here than in Fleet Street.

November 19. Hot spot of the day: met Mr. and Mrs. X at lunch in the Café Royal. Though the lunch was as lousy as usual, the conversation between Mrs. X and myself was most interesting. She is rather pleasant to say the least. She has been here 2½ years, speaks English perfectly apart from an attractive

---

* Restaurant food and price restrictions don't start until June 1940. From then on, restaurants may no longer serve both a fish and a meat dish at the same meal. Later on, diners are restricted to three-course meals (dessert is counted as a third course). Source: "British War Time Food" in www.cooksinfo.com

little accent, and Dutch abominably, and has never met any Dutch people in this country. The poor thing—I rather liked her, as you might gather—is married to one of those moustachy, insipid-looking Englishmen, who added just three words to the conversation, of which two were "darling."

To Jan's surprise, not only is he seeking information from experts, but soon he too is regarded as an expert—by those whom he considers his superiors. He is surprised at his new status.

> **November 30.** A senior person at our Economics Department came down this morning to show me a broadcast which he had prepared, and asked for comment. I gave it! What a topsy-turvy world I am living in.

Although Jan is no longer a journalist per se, his responsibilities include a fair amount of writing, at times under his own byline and at times anonymously as a speechwriter for Dutch government officials.

> **January 24, 1941.** Pelt came in this morning, and, having seen a good show in the *Times*, offered his congratulations with my work.

> **January 29.** Last night I wrote a damned good paragraph, which we put out on the tape and was prominently displayed in all evening editions, and sent out to Reuters World Service.

March 7. At the office things are going along nicely. The *Catholic Herald* has published my letter, the *Universe* runs a front-page Dutch feature, and so does the *Tablet*. All excellent publicity.

March 11. Gerbrandy has asked me to discuss his speech for a luncheon tomorrow at the Royal Empire Society. I had a big hand in preparing a speech for Prince Bernard, also for that luncheon.

The speech, which Jan drafts for Prince Bernard, clearly reflects that, at the time, the Dutch government has a sense of equality with England in terms of world power. This changes a year later, in March 1942, when the Dutch East Indies surrender to the Japanese.[34]

March 19 [Excerpt from Prince Bernard's Speech to the Royal Empire Society]. The Royal Empire Society is today honoring my country, which, like yours, is proud of its empire. Queen Wilhelmina's subjects in the great island empire in the East, The Netherlands East Indies, and her people in the Dutch territories of the western hemisphere, Curacao and Suriname, may be far away, but they have heard the call and they are not failing to respond.

Commemorating the Bombing of Rotterdam

A major component of Jan's work can best be described as public relations. One project with which he is very pleased is a commemoration of the May 1940 bombing of Rotterdam.

February 26. Have now the most damning photo of "cleared up" Rotterdam ever. You will not believe your eyes. Apart from the *Groote Kerk* there is nothing, and absolutely nothing for about one square mile covered by the photo. The *Groote Markt, Hoogstraat, Korte Hoogstraat* are recognizable only by that little stream of water, which used to be near our old office. It is really frightening. Rotterdam can never be forgotten.

May 7. I have ordered a Mass for Holland on May 10 and to which I have invited ministers and people. Did I tell you that Father P. is saying the Mass that I have one soldier and one *marechaussee* [military police] serving, that two ministers are coming, that all Catholics of detachment London are being given time to come, and that the Dutch Grail girls are also turning up.* May be a reasonable attendance after all.

May 10. My service in Farm Street [a Jesuit church in the Mayfair District] has been a great success. There were over 100 people, which is more than I expected. It was a fine sight, and many thanked me for having thought of arranging this service on my own bat. I still have to pay the stipend, but one minister phoned me today, that I should let him at least share.

---

* The Grail Movement was started in 1921 by a Dutch Jesuit as a social action initiative for Catholic laywomen. It has since expanded worldwide and membership is open to women of all faiths. Source: "History of the Grail Movement." http://thegrail.org

Rotterdam has been brought in the limelight again. This morning's march through the town by the Dutch military band was a great success, and this afternoon's main service at the ruins of Austin Friars, where the old Dutch church stood—there is really nothing left of it—was extremely impressive.* I hope you will listen to the broadcasts tonight of both *Radio Oranje* and the BBC.

Have reason to be extremely pleased with our publicity. I was able to have a report published in the London evening papers, and have an item broadcast to Holland in the Dutch program. A number of papers carried leaders or feature articles. *The Daily Express* as usual refused. The *Daily Telegraph,* also a difficult one, had a combined Dutch-Belgian story yesterday and two photos of Rotterdam today.

May 12. Our publicity has been enormous this weekend. Nothing like it has ever been produced. Leading articles all over the shop and photos as never before. A pity you cannot see more than just the *Express*. This morning's *Times* was again a Dutch edition!

---

* German bombs destroy the Austin Friars church the night of October 15, 1940. The church's Dutch roots date back to 1550, when King Edward VI gave the church to Dutch Protestants fleeing religious persecution. Source: Henri van der Zee, *In Ballingschap. De Nederlandse Kolonie in Engeland [1940-1945]* (Amsterdam: De Bezige Bij, 2005), 128ff.

Radio Oranje

In July 1940, the BBC agrees to transmit Dutch-language broadcasts over its senders. Initially there are two such programs, *Radio Oranje* for the general population and, for seamen, the *Brandaris*—named after the oldest lighthouse in The Netherlands. The name Oranje derives from the fact that the Dutch royals are members and rulers of the House of Oranje Nassau. The color orange is therefore as much an emblem of Dutch patriotism as its red, white, and blue flag. These broadcasts allow the government to send messages of hope and encouragement to citizens of occupied Holland, correct the misinformation published by the Nazi-controlled Dutch papers, and send coded messages to the Dutch underground.

For a while, Jan provides text for a number of *Radio Oranje* broadcasts.

> **October 17, 1940.** My wireless speech, which I had written some time ago, has been approved by the Economics Department. They want me to broadcast it myself.

On at least one occasion, he is on the air.

> **March 28, 1941.** Did you recognize my voice? I am anxiously looking forward to tomorrow morning when the speech is being rebroadcast. The first time one is always a bit nervy, though Jan and Toos have not noticed a trace of an accent. When I learned this morning that my speech would be going out tonight, I suggested that I should read it myself. I

was ready to go through the excitement of facing the mike myself, thinking of the possibility of my people recognizing my voice, and *vrouwtje* being pleased to hear me broadcast. Things went well, though I was rather scared of making a mess of it.

Jan's voice contributions are limited to *Radio Oranje's* start-up phase. In 1942, Pelt combines the somewhat dull *Radio Oranje* with the considerably less staid *Brandaris* radio service. The new *Radio Oranje* is put under the direction of Henk van den Broek.

Vrij Nederland, an Independent Weekly

During his first few years as a press officer, Jan does some freelance writing for the Dutch-language weekly, *Vrij Nederland* [The Free Netherlands].* Although closely allied with the work of the RPD, *Vrij Nederland* remains independent and not part of the government structure. The editor is Marcus Blankenstein. Jan's letters indicate that he does his writing during the long evenings when he feels sufficiently safe to spend the night in the Hazebroek house rather than in the shelter. The Hazebroeks, on the other hand, retire to the shelter every evening as this is an easier routine for their children.

Jan is pleased with the additional exposure and the extra income.

---

* *Vrij Nederland* is the brainchild of W.S. Boas, who before the war worked in the publicity department of a Dutch newspaper, the *Telegraaf.* Having fled to London, Boas writes the government and suggests a Dutch paper to repudiate German propaganda and to inform Dutch civilians. Pelt likes the idea and obtains start-up funding from Paul Rijkens, the London-based vice president of Unilever and president of The Netherlands Publishing Company. Source: Van der Zee. *In Ballingschap,* op. cit., 107-109.

October 25. This week's *Vrij Nederland* carried quite a good deal again from me. All to the good.

October 31. Received a check for £15 from *Vrij Nederland*. Very useful. Was able to get into the good books of the management of Unilever with some information which was very useful to them. Cannot do any harm. I have come to the house after my supper (I don't like the idea very much of eating sandwiches in the shelter night after night, but Jan and Toos feel more comfortable there) to write my next week's market report for *Vrij Nederland*. I must keep that up, *coûte que coûte*. This week's issue carries again 1½ pages of my dope. I must get the old numbers out of my flat to store them away. I feel it would pay if we had a spare set, in view of the premium that may be paid later on in Holland. And it is rather a nice collection of my work, since I have not kept all my scripts.

What Jan sometimes describes as scrappy little articles, "money for jam," are clearly well regarded and recognized as being written by him—even though they do not carry his byline.

January 25, 1942. Pelt came in late yesterday afternoon. We talked generally about things, during which he remarked that *Vrij Nederland* had asked him to release me for a permanent *Vrij Nederland* editorial position (as editorial administrator with considerable powers!). Pelt had refused. It would have meant more money, but I don't think I would have accepted.

March 27. Tomorrow I am lunching with the managing director of *Vrij Nederland*. I should stand him a good luncheon, bad luck. After all, I earn about £150 a year on his paper, a very useful sideline, worth spending something to keep the contact warm.*

An Unexpected Job Offer

The following letter is undated but was written after Jan's first *Radio Oranje* broadcast in March 1941 and prior to the end of the Blitz in May 1941.

Spring 1941. *Vrouwtje*, the following is secret, in other words for the time being not to be discussed with the Keegans or anyone else. Minister Steenberghe has been approached by his Secretary General and by his economics expert, who, both non-Catholics, had advised the Minister, each independently, that the Minister should ask me to join their department as economics expert! Mr. Steenberghe also mentioned that he had heard at the cabinet meeting that Minister Van Kleffens mentioned my name in connection with a foreign post (don't get worried until you've finished this letter), probably New York, to look after the economic

---

* It is not clear for how long Jan continues writing for *Vrij Nederland*, but he appears to have stopped in late 1942.

side of publicity and diplomatic information. Poor Jantje, two ministers fishing for me. Who would ever have thought it possible?

You will want to know what I think of it all. It is difficult to say. My heart remains in my present press work. I should not dream of leaving my *schatje* behind on this island and move to New York. But if it were a matter of a flying visit for a reasonably short time, the matter might be discussable. Van Kleffens' offer—if it comes off, which is not quite definite— would put me in a position which I feel I can tackle in one way or another. I would be attached to our embassy as press attaché. After the war, I shall not find men who would look at me as an intruder. The position would be retained in America, England, or some other leading country, as we need new men trained for this particular work. For journalistic purposes, and reason of safety of future status, Van Kleffens' offer looks sound.

On the other hand, joining the Economic Ministry with Steenberghe would mean an end to my journalistic activities. And what would happen at the end of the war? His offer—if I accept—would bring me in Holland into a class of exclusive university men who might find that I only got in that position through sheer force of special circumstances and through the fact that I, as a Catholic, had been privileged by a Catholic minister.

Steenberghe explained that he personally had had an eye on me for some time and that he felt happy that two non-Catholics and Van Kleffens [also a non-Catholic] had similar views. In this connection, I have to tell *vrouwtje* the following, which no doubt is as interesting to her as to me. Steenberghe has all praise for my articles in *Vrij Nederland*, referred again to my clear broadcast address, and made it clear that he did not like the idea at all of dragging me away from my press officer's job, where—as he said—I was doing valuable work, especially as a Catholic with sound ideas which counteracted the strong influences of certain left and Jewish influences.

Kindjelief, I have never been honoured so much in all my life. I want to share all this with my *vrouwtje*, who so fully wants to share all.

To the Dutch at that time, one's religion and political affiliation are pretty much one and the same. The underpinning of Dutch pre-war—and for that matter, post-war—society consists of four religious or ideological "pillars": Protestant (non-Catholic Christian), Catholic, social-democratic, and liberal. There is no Jewish pillar; at the time, Jewish writers and authors were generally associated with the liberal or socialist pillars.

Each pillar has its own political parties and associated schools, youth groups, sport clubs, and even unions.[35] Thus, members of one group rarely meet with one another in social or other settings. This is the experience that most of the Dutch refugees and government officials have brought to London. Jan's reflection on Steenberghe's job offer makes sense within the context of this four-pillared system. He fears that some may view the job offer has having been made on the basis of his Catholicism.

Steenberghe's concern about "certain left and Jewish influences" reflects the existing conflict between of the government in London and the Jewish intellectuals who in Holland had not been part of the government establishment—a conflict confirmed by Dutch historian Louis de Jong in a chapter on anti-Semitism within the Dutch government in London.[36]

As it turns out, Jan accepts neither job offer. Or rather, it is not clear whether Van Kleffens' offer ever materializes. Jan may have turned down Steenberghe's offer because it would not have been feasible to bring his young family to the States.

After the Blitz

Finding a house in the general vicinity of London proves to be no easy task. Jan is delighted when Kate and Hannah Whitelaw, relatives of Marie's older half-siblings, tell him of a cottage for rent in Wraysbury, a small village on the Thames. Jan visits the cottage in mid-summer 1941. He signs the lease, not daring to wait to consult Marie—having missed several possibilities because he hesitated just a little too long. The family moves to Wraysbury in late summer 1941.

CHAPTER IV

FAMILY LIFE IN WRAYSBURY
June 1941 to September 1944

In midsummer 1941, Jan first visits Cheyne Cottage, the little house in Wraysbury that will become the home where he will live with Marie and the children, and from where he will be commuting to the Press Office in London. In a letter to Marie he expresses both his enthusiasm and misgivings:

> **Undated. Summer 1941.** I saw the cottage, and though I found a great many things which still worry me, I took it on the spot, to prevent other aspirants beating me to it again. The cottage has the pokiest of poky windows. Never seen anything like it. It has one small, very small dining room, a little larger lounge, a fine kitchen (electric stove—boiler—larder—coal place—cupboard space—draining boards on both sides of the sink). That's downstairs. Upstairs (everything is so low that I almost have to bend when I get through my new home), I have one bedroom (low and dark, little window covered by a

mass of leaves from a tree), two more even smaller bedrooms, one bathroom with WC (modern).

There is the loveliest garden you could imagine, at the back—lovely flowers—a fairly large lawn—then the vegetable garden. How to upkeep all that, I don't know. The owner has a gardener once in two weeks. I should have him at least once a week, but he does not seem to have more time. I intend to do something myself, and trust that you will help me, if we can get some tools!

The house is hidden by lots of bushes and trees. A good thing too, since it is nothing to look at from the front. There are lots of trees in front, plus a small garden. There is water off the main. We have a cesspool. If it is full up, you phone the district counsellor, who seems to come and take it away. We in the country don't mind that so much as you townspeople.

There are a few shops, but main shopping should be done in Staines or Slough. Bus services I think to Staines only 10 minutes. The cottage is a 20-minute walk from the station. Communications to London are lousy. I dread the idea, but I am willing to put up with it, if you come and join me and make the best of things. It takes 40 minutes from Waterloo station to Wraysbury, at least 20 minutes to get from Piccadilly to Waterloo—a train every hour—three in the top hours—and 20 minutes of walking at the other end. So at least 80 minutes! Poor me in the winter months!

We shall be only ten minutes' walk from the river, where owner and little son went swimming today. Boating available. One good pub. No Catholic church, but service every Sunday in the hall at the back of that pub! We are going to be in the wilds. Village looks very neat and clean. Treesje will love the fields (also at the back of my cottage). Saw many fine kids, always an agreeable sign. No shelter. Also a good sign. (These people have two kids and have done without.) There is a telephone—a great blessing.

It is comparatively safe there, though shrapnel has been known to drop in the lane. You will come. I know. And I trust you will from the moment you receive this news start making all necessary arrangements. I hope I have not painted a too-rosy picture of the cottage. Here was a chance. I took it, fearing that any dillydallying would again make me miss the boat. You will help me arrange the moving and planning of the place, won't you?

Though it is a compact little place, I have asked the owner's weekly woman to continue with us. You can be sure the place will be left to you in a clean state. I have also asked the owner to register us for coal for the winter. Coal is going to be the bugbear this winter. If I can find a saw, we can have plenty of logs!

Schatjelief, I dare not be too enthusiastic about things as I am not so sure that you can fall in with my momentous decision wholeheartedly. Of course you will make the best of things. And it can be a nice place, despite its poky windows and its very tiny rooms. Thank God, there are plenty of big cupboards to put a lot of things away. So our new place need not look cramped and full of rubbish.

I hope to give you a happy little home. I am so thrilled at heart that I am inclined to forget that waiting a little longer might have brought me a nicer and bigger place. But the die has been cast. I am expecting you, my love, back to my home. Whatever snags you may have to face, I'll do my utmost to make you happy here.

Family Life in Wraysbury

Cheyne Cottage is the home that Treesje and Colette remember when they think of their early childhood. It doesn't take long for Jan and Marie to become part of the village and develop good friends, in particular Tony and Betty Hanefey, whose daughters Mary and Ann are about the same age as Treesje and Colette, and Rémi Baert, a Belgian diplomat who, with his Dutch-born wife Toos and three little daughters, has also found safe refuge in the village.

Marie with Colette in the garden of Cheyne Cottage.
Wraysbury. Fall 1941.

Hannah Whitelaw's bungalow is across the lane. "Auntie" Hannah is a major help to Marie, always ready to watch the children, who look on her as a surrogate grandmother—all the more so after the unexpected death of Marie's mother, of a coronary thrombosis, on July 27, 1943. Until then, "Gallo" (as the children call Marie's mother) visits often—the train from London to Wraysbury being so much easier than the long journey to Taunton. Marie's sister Agnes and half-brother Laurent are happy as well that the young family now lives within reasonable distance of the city.

Marie loves the cottage—especially the flower and vegetable gardens. With the help of a part-time gardener, she grows most of the family's vegetables. Jan will later boast to his children of his efforts to get up before the neighbors to collect horse dung for fertilizer. Fruit trees provide the family with plenty of pears as well as plums. A field separates the garden from a lovely old Norman church dating to the 12th century.[37] The surrounding countryside is ideal for Marie's daily walks with the children to the village, across the fields, down to the Thames, or to the nearby old manor farm.

Jan is happy to be living with Marie and the children, despite the daily trek into the city. He is now truly part of the family—coming home in the evening in time for a light supper with Marie. Treesje and Colette are by then asleep—Marie adheres to the then-customary 6:30 bedtime for the children. Jan and Marie often manage a game of bridge with new friends, especially the Baerts. When weather and work allow, Jan enjoys a weekend game of tennis with neighbors.

His commute eases significantly when he can obtain a ride home with Pelt, who, with his wife and family, has moved to nearby Farnham Common. Mrs. Pelt adopts the young family—so much so that she invites them to stay with her family for several weeks prior to and after the birth of Jan and Marie's third child. This time it's a boy, born July 10, 1942, in nearby Slough. His full name is Johannes Franciscus, but he is known as Jantje or, for a while, as "Baby John."

Marie and Jantje. Wraysbury. Fall 1942.

The little cottage in the country also welcomes visitors from London, who are only too happy to get out of the city for the day. One of these visitors is Jan's friend and colleague Herman de Man, who in the summer of 1943 photographs Jan and Marie with their three little ones.

Jan, Marie and the children. Wraysbury. Summer 1943.
Photos by Herman de Man.

Contact with Family Abroad

There are few letters, describing the day-to-day life of Jan and Marie's stay in Wraysbury. What do remain are records of their efforts to contact family abroad: Jan's parents and siblings in Holland and Marie's far-flung family in France and Egypt.*

One obstacle to wartime communication with family abroad is the Emergency Powers Defense Act. It requires that every press and commercial, and even private messages leaving Britain, whether by mail, cable, wireless, or telephone, be approved by censors.

A Dutch section of the Red Cross's Prisoners of War Central Agency is set up in May 1940, to arrange an interchange of news between The Netherlands and the Dutch who had taken refuge abroad, including in Britain.[38] The process can take months. For instance, in May 1940, Jan and Marie try to find out whether Jan's parents and siblings survived the bombing of Rotterdam. The form for this request is called "Enquiry for Missing Relatives." The response that all are well does not arrive until five months later, in late October.

As of 1941, it is through the Red Cross that Marie, her mother, and her siblings Laurent and Agnes communicate with family in France. The one-page Red Cross form (on which the message may consist of no more than 25 words) goes from the English War Organization of the British Red Cross to the British censors; from there to the Geneva Red Cross; then from Geneva to the country of destination. The same form with the response written on

---

* Marie's French grandfather worked in Egypt as a chief of dragging operations for the Suez Canal. His six children were all born there. Some, including Marie's mother, returned to France in adulthood; others remained in Egypt. Marie is very close to the Egyptian branch of the family, especially those cousins who used to gather in the summer at the home of their grandmother in Voiron, France.

the reverse side (again in 25 words or less) is routed through the Geneva and the British censors before being returned to the original sender.

On at least two occasions, Jan manages to bypass the Red Cross system. On December 12, 1941, he tells Marie that he was able to send the news of Colette's birth to his parents via diplomatic channels.

> **December 12, 1941.** In confidence—as far as the Keegans and all others are concerned—V. gave me, on my request, a Portuguese postcard to send home to my people from Portugal, via the diplomatic bag. Mind you, that is a special privilege and should not be discussed.

In October 1943, he writes a congratulatory note to one of his sisters, Len, on the occasion of her marriage in May of that year. Len saves this letter along with the original envelope postmarked *Lisboa*—with a Lisbon return address. For censorship reasons, nothing in the letter gives any sense of Jan's whereabouts.

Letters to and from Egypt are written on airgraphs. This system, invented in the 1930s by the Eastman Kodak Company, was instituted in 1941 between England and Egypt to reduce the weight of letters. The forms on which letters are written are photographed and then mailed to the country of destination as negatives on a roll of film. At their destination, these are printed out on photographic paper and distributed to the addressee. The photographs are very small, about two by three inches, and difficult to read.[39]

Jan's Wartime Travel

Living with Marie in Wraysbury, Jan no longer needs to write letters to Marie—except during two short trips, one to Ireland and one to Scotland. In May 1942, he accompanies Prince Bernard, Speekenbrink, and other Dutch officials to openings of Dutch exhibits in Belfast and Portrush, Ireland. The trip to Belfast may well have been the first time Jan travelled by plane. It appears to have been a very small plane—the kind that includes parachutes for passengers in case of an emergency evacuation.

In August 1943, he travels to Edinburgh, Scotland, where Prince Bernard, Gerbrandy, and Pelt officiate at the opening of a Dutch exhibit at the Scottish National Gallery.

> **August 7, 1943.** Edinburgh is a charming town. Quaint and clean. Too many people and no quiet place to relax make things rather tiring. The Scots seem to be rather fed up with all those blasted foreigners who have invaded their country. No wonder, considering the number of Scot-Polish babies born since the beginning of the hostilities.[40]

> **August 9.** Pelt's press conference has been a great success. I should have liked to share in the honor since I prepared all the material. All day I have been preparing Gerbrandy's speech for tomorrow. Just when it was such a beautiful day.

> **August 12.** I am interrupted once more, and I intended to tell you all about Monday's functions: of the luncheon offered by the British Council to

Prince Bernard, Gerbrandy, and ten other Dutch guests; of the dinner Gerbrandy and the Dutch offered the British Council; of the invitation by the Dutch officers of a submarine to come and have a drink in their " home." I seldom saw a finer body of men. You would have fallen for each of them.

Jan enjoys these breaks from routine and would love to be assigned additional travel abroad. He is delighted when, on September 22, Pelt raises the possibility that Jan may go to Portugal and from there on to South Africa. Nothing comes of this, and when Jan raises the issue, Pelt replies that there is no one to replace him in London.

Finally, in March 1944, Pelt asks Jan to visit Lisbon and Madrid. Jan is delighted. Plans proceed to the point where Gerbrandy approves the travel plans, and Van Kleffens the travel costs. A mere four days later, a disappointed Jan learns that all diplomatic travel has been curtailed.

CHAPTER V

PLANNING POST-WAR RECONSTRUCTION
January 1943 to December 1944

In January 1943, Jan starts a diary in which he jots down his thoughts, observations, and experiences—in an abbreviated style, jumping back and forth between English and Dutch. This diary provides an overview of the Dutch government's preparation for eventual liberation from the German occupation and describes Jan's ever-evolving role as a press officer.

Post-war Planning

By early 1943, major changes are taking place within the exiled Dutch government as a result of the increasingly realistic hope that within a year or so Germany will be defeated. It therefore becomes increasingly important for The Netherlands and other occupied nations to start planning the post-war reconstruction of their countries' physical and administrative infrastructure. One reason for this thrust toward post-war planning is the January 1943 surrender of the heretofore-indomitable German army to the Russians at the battle of Stalingrad.[41]

For The Netherlands and other western European countries, plans for the eventual post-war reconstruction take place in conjunction with the efforts of other nations, including the United States, which entered the war in December 1941. Although the United States had initially declared, this neutrality ends on December 7, 1941, when the Japanese bomb Pearl Harbor.

Within days, the United States declares war on Japan, and Germany declares war on the United States. Up until then, the United States had hoped to aid the occupied European countries without having to declare war on Germany. For instance, in August 1941, while still maintaining U.S. neutrality, President Roosevelt had met with Winston Churchill in Newfoundland to develop the Atlantic Charter—setting principles for the post-war reconstruction of Europe. In January 1943, Roosevelt and Churchill reconvene, this time in Casablanca, to finalize Allied strategic plans against the Germans—their "Blueprint for Victory."[42]

In December 1943, General Dwight D. Eisenhower is appointed the Allied Supreme Commander.[43] His command becomes known as SHAEF (Supreme Headquarters Allied Expeditionary Forces). It is SHAEF that prepares and eventually leads the initial rebuilding and civil affairs of the occupied nations once they are liberated.

Planning Post-War Press and Censorship

In January 1943 the Dutch Minister of War establishes a military authority, the *Militair Gezag*—under the direction of General Hendrik Kruls—to run the country immediately after liberation.[44] Members of the *Militair Gezag* are to be trained to restore order and start the reconstruction process—the training and the reconstruction to be conducted in conjunction with SHAEF. General Kruls assigns Pelt the responsibility of the press and information services of the *Militair Gezag*.

Jan is not involved in the start-up phase of the Press and Information Services (Section XI) of the *Militair Gezag*. In fact, early on, he notes in his diary that he is not sure what his role will be, if any. In October 1943, he learns that a colleague, Jimmy Huizinga, has been assigned the preparation for the post-war Section XI activities. Huizinga, like Jan, was a Dutch correspondent living in London when the war broke out, working as a journalist for the Dutch daily the *Nieuwe Rotterdamse Courant*. His background and experience, however, are different. Prior to coming to London, Huizinga studied in the United States. He also spent a year at the beginning of the war in the Dutch Information Office in New York before being transferred back to London.

Jan's specific post-war role is unclear at first. Pelt has yet to decide whether Jan will be active in press censorship or news distribution activities of the *Militair Gezag*.

To ensure unrestricted travel in liberated areas, as well as access to logistics, supplies, and other support from Allied military forces, it becomes necessary to militarize civilians such as Jan, who will be sent to The Netherlands once it is free.[45] Thus in January 1944, Jan and a number of his colleagues participate in a week of military training at the Dutch army base in Wolverhampton, northwest of Birmingham. On his first day, he writes Marie:

January 17, 1944. It is pleasant to be away from my office desk for a few days. I have turned right, when left was ordered. I have been called to attention by the *Kommandant,* but on the whole I have managed quite nicely on my first morning. Tell Treesje that her Papa is now a real soldier.

In June 1944, Jan notes in his diary that Pelt considers appointing Jan as chief representative of Section XI in the first wave of *Militair Gezag* personnel being sent to Holland. He adds that Pelt finds it difficult to decide between him and Huizinga. Huizinga, because of his involvement in the initial planning phase, knows about the workings of the *Militair Gezag* and the various sections, but Jan is more familiar with Holland. In the end, Pelt decides that Jan will be in charge of censorship and Huizinga in charge of news distribution. Jan is disappointed—he fears that if he is no longer involved in news distribution, he will not be in the running for a good position in the government's Press and Information Services after the war.

In July, Jan officially becomes a member of the Militair Gezag. His identity card indicates that he is on active duty in The Netherlands—something which, it is hoped, will become a reality in the coming months.

In preparation for his assignment in post-war Holland, Jan becomes immersed in the censorship training provided by the Ministry of Information—the British government agency in charge of British press censorship. So far his work has focused on good publicity for the Dutch with the occasional suppression of negative publicity. Censorship directives are considerably more structured and

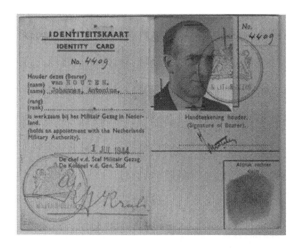

Jan's identity card for the *Militair Gezag*.
Date of issue: July 1, 1944.

stringent. They require the publicity media to "suppress publication of material that might imperil the war effort."[46]

The censorship training follows SHAEF guidelines. Jan's training
occurs in the British Ministry of Information. No doubt at some
point he is given a copy of the SHAEF press censorship "bible,"
a 200-page mimeographed document containing the censorship policy of British, Canadian, and U.S. forces in the European
theater.[47]

Ongoing Press Office Responsibilities

Jan's censorship and related training are preparations for the future.
Until then, his primary role remains that of press officer: briefing

and assisting British and foreign correspondents. One of these is Martha Hemingway from *Colliers Magazine*.*

> **December 17, 1943 [Diary entry].** [Hemingway] is a typical American journalist. Is here for *Colliers*. Wants to go aboard the Dutch sea torpedoes, speak with the Queen, etc. We are her "darlings."

> **January 5, 1944 [Diary entry].** Mrs. Hemingway phoned. Yesterday she visited the Queen: "Darling, she is lovely."

But mostly Jan is kept busy with problematic press issues. His job is to make sure that media stories support the war effort and maintain the morale of the civilian population in Holland. This means judicious selection—and occasional suppression—of facts. In several instances, the request to repress certain news, at least temporarily, comes directly from the Queen.

Media Reports on the Bombing of the Queen's Home

Between January and March, the German *Luftwaffe* carries out what becomes known as the Baby Blitz or the Little Blitz—"a final and concentrated effort by the *Luftwaffe* ... mostly aimed at London. Typically the Baby Blitz raids release heavy loads of

---

* Martha Hemingway, née Gelhorn, was Ernest Hemingway's third wife. In 1940 she became a European war correspondent for *Colliers*. Martha was the only woman and one of the few correspondents to come ashore (reportedly as a stow-away on a hospital ship) at Omaha Beach on D-Day. Source: http://www.biography.com/people/martha-gellhorn-20903335#synopsis

incendiaries."[48] On February 23, 1944, the *Daily Mirror* reports that the Queen's house has been bombed.[49]

> **February 23 [Diary entry].** Report from *Daily Mirror:* Queen's house damaged. Two guards killed. This was first intimation to R.V.D. Got in touch with [the Queen's staff]. Confirmed [that bombing occurred], but [found out that] Queen did not want anything published. Asked D.A.D. [Deputy Assistant Director of Censorship] if such report was submitted. Their answer: "To be held 28 days."

Later that day, Jan learns that the news has passed censorship after all, and that *The Daily Mirror* carries the story.

> **February 24 [Diary entry].** [The Queen's staff] insisted that nothing should be said. When it became known that Boston had broadcast the ANEP/*The Mirror* "report," *Radio Oranje* was allowed to say something.

Possible reasons for attempting to suppress such an apparently newsworthy story are to keep the news from the Germans and to prevent Dutch civilians and Allies from thinking that the Queen is not safe.

Responding to Controversial Press

A few days later (February 26), a rare Saturday at home for Jan is interrupted by another crisis. The weekly publication *The New Statesman* publishes an article entitled "Anglo-Dutch

Union" that creates quite a stir.⁵⁰ The author, W. van Leer, is a Dutch engineer who has been in England since 1937. Van Leer proposes that after the war "British military occupational forces should take over the administration of Holland." His argument is that the Dutch administration in England no longer represents the interests of the new Holland. He describes the Prime Minister as "a fanatical Calvinistic professor of law" and the Dutch administration in London as "a lightweight team of careerist politicians and civil servants." It is his belief that the proposed Dutch military administration of Holland will not be accepted by the Dutch people.

Frenzied days of phone calls with Pelt, Poelhekke from the RPD, and Meijer Sluijser from *Vrij Nederland* follow the publication of Van Leer's article. The final decision is that Pelt and Dirk de Man will ask Burger, the then Minister charged with post-war planning, to write a letter to Kingsley Martin, the editor of the *New Statesman*.

> **February 29 [Diary entry].** Learned that the South
> Africa news agency had cabled part of *New Statesman*
> article to South Africa. Passed it on to Pelt with sug-
> gestion to send article by Burger for background.
> Lunched with Sluijser and again discussed Van Leer's
> article. Sluijser's view is that Van Leer's statement
> is upheld by many escapees, that the cause of this
> feeling can be found in the Queen's criticism of the
> Cabinet, etc. The Queen is not pleased.

On March 7, Jan reports that the Dutch Foreign Office has received a request to place a short newsreel in *The Voice* about a February bombing of Nijmegen by the Americans "On the advice of the Foreign Office did not do this." The February 22 bombing occurred when Allied planes mistake the city for a German one. More than 750 people are killed, and there is significant damage to the city center.[51]

In May 1944, Jan is kept busy trying to undo the damage caused by Jacques Gans, a disgruntled staff member of *Radio Oranje* and outspoken critic of the exiled government. The first sign of a problem occurs when Gerbrandy arranges a lunch for *Radio Oranje* staff. Gans refuses the invitation because, in his opinion, the news that the Dutch are broadcasting to Holland is nothing but propaganda. Also, he doesn't approve of the role that the *Militair Gezag* will have following liberation. Shortly thereafter, Gans sends out 700 copies of a statement saying that the Dutch government has become an authoritarian regime. When copies find their way to the U.S. State Department in Washington, the Dutch ambassador is asked why the Dutch have rejected democracy. In London, Van Kleffens has to reassure the American ambassador, Anthony J. Drexel Biddle, Jr., when the latter asks how many Nazis there are in the Dutch government.[52]

Press reports on Prince Bernard and the Queen

The British view Prince Bernard, the Queen's charming son-in-law—by birth a German—with some distrust.[*] In many ways the Prince is the *enfant terrible* of the Dutch colony. His womanizing and other exploits are kept from the Queen, who is a strong supporter of the Prince. Examples of incidents that must be kept from the press and from the Queen include the Prince's

---

[*] The prince's German name is Bernhard. However, Jan uses the Dutch spelling: Bernard.

July 1 (post D-Day) flight to Normandy and a July 10 visit to the Pope in Rome. The prince's visit to the Pope occurs less than a month after Holland renews diplomatic relations with the Vatican.

The Queen does not want news that reflects negatively on her son-in-law to be reported by the press. She does not accept Pelt's position that because of the freedom of the press in the United States and Britain, it is not always possible to suppress less favorable news. Things come to a head in August 1944, when the book *Queen Wilhelmina, Mother of The Netherlands* is published, stating that as a youth in Germany, Prince Bernard was a member of a Nazi organization.[53] Both the Queen and the Prince are furious. Not only does Pelt not prevent the publication of this book, but he also fails to stop *Vrij Nederland* from purchasing 1,000 copies.

At one point, the Queen considers appointing the Prince as head of the *Militair Gezag* but backs down because of lack of support from her cabinet and the War Minister. Moreover, Eisenhower does not consider him to have the necessary experience.[54] In September, however, the Queen appoints Prince Bernard as commander of the Dutch Forces of the Interior—a newly established force consisting of wartime resistance groups.

Cabinet Crises

Jan's position in the Press Office gives him a ringside seat to the challenges faced by the Dutch government in preparing for the return to Holland. As early as May 1944, he writes, "*Het rommelt in de kolonie* [It rumbles in the colony]."

His diary records major conflict between the Queen and several ministers, including the Prime Minister. The Queen and Gerbrandy do not see eye to eye on post-war reconstruction plans. At the start of the war, they had been in total accord regarding plans to resist the Germans. However, the Queen, who has enjoyed greater power during her time in London than before the war, advocates a new system in which greater power is accorded to the monarchy. She also advocates greater inclusion of the leaders of Dutch resistance groups.

Jan is all the more aware of these various conflicts because he now finds himself regularly having lunch with and even being consulted by Cabinet members. In his 1940 and 1941 letters to Marie, he had reported with certain awe the occasional lunch with a minister or his representative. These lunches are now the norm.

Another indication of Jan's increased visibility occurs on June 2, 1944, when Prime Minister Gerbrandy asks Jan whether he would consider a place on the Extraordinary Advisory Council.* Cabinet members fully support Jan's appointment. Jan, however, turns down the offer, as he doesn't feel justified in taking on this additional responsibility. He believes there may be some conflict of interest between the two very distinct roles of press officer and government advisor.

At one point, Jan is even considered as the successor to Pelt as the head of Section XI of the *Militair Gezag*, for, although Pelt has the

---

* The Dutch government formed this Advisory Council in 1942 as a means to obtain some form of citizen feedback Source: Louis de Jong. *Het Koninkrijk der Nederlanden in de Tweede Wereldoorlog. Londen.* Deel. 9a. (The Hague, Staatsuitgeverij, 1979), 375-378.

full confidence and support of Van Kleffens and Gerbrandy, the Queen is less taken with him.

In August 1944, Gerbrandy, fearing that the Queen will not sign the formal appointment of Pelt as head of Section XI of the *Militair Gezag*, informs Jan that he has discussed the matter with Kruls and Van Heuven Goedhart and they have decided to submit Jan's name as the new head of Section XI. Huizinga and Van den Broek have also been considered, but Jan is the final candidate. Jan responds that he cannot accept this position. Jan reports that Gerbrandy replies: "Then I shall order you to accept."

On August 11, Jan meets again with Gerbrandy (who has since consulted with Van Kleffens, who has just returned from vacation). At Van Kleffens' suggestion, Gerbrandy decides to wait until the last minute to submit Pelt's name to the Queen. If Pelt is not accepted, "then Van Houten." But at the last minute, the Queen confirms Pelt's appointment.

D-Day, 1944

The liberation of western Europe begins on June 6, 1944 with the landing of 155,000 Allied troops on the beaches of Normandy. D-Day's success leads to the gradual liberation of all of France.[55] Paris is liberated on August 25, and De Gaulle (who since April 1944 has been the head of the Free French Armed Forces) enters Paris on August 26 and walks in triumph down the Champs Elysées.[56] War correspondents arrive in Paris with the first Allied troops that enter the city.

Expecting that the Allies will soon liberate Belgium and The Netherlands, the Dutch government readies the first contingent of the *Militair Gezag*. On August 25, Jan is recalled from his annual holiday, which he is spending at home with Marie and the children. On August 31, 1944, he is sworn in as a temporary reserve captain of the Dutch army.

By early September 1944, the allies have crossed into Belgium. As soon as Brussels and Antwerp are liberated (on September 3 and 4, respectively), the Belgian government returns from its exile in London.[57] On September 5, Jan receives word from the *Militair Gezag* that he must be ready for deployment at a moment's notice. Five days later, the Dutch government, anticipating that the Allied forces will continue their successful surge north and that The Netherlands will be liberated next, moves the offices of the *Militair Gezag* to Brussels.

Ever since his August 25 swearing in ceremony, Jan has been preparing to leave—even though he doesn't know quite when this will happen. Preparations include drinks with friends and visits to London with Marie to get all paperwork in order, including a lunch with colleagues on August 31 and, on September 2, a meeting with Gerbrandy—also with Marie.

On September 14, the censorship division of the *Militair Gezag* is moved to Brussels. Jan's deployment, although anticipated, is still unexpected and sudden. He leaves from his office in London, without having had the chance to say goodbye to Marie and the children in Wraysbury.

Captain J.A. van Houten. London. September 1944.
This is the photo the children kissed goodnight
during Jan's prolonged absence.

CHAPTER VI

PRESS CENSOR IN BRABANT
September to December 1944

On September 14, 1944, Jan flies from England to Brussels, Belgium, to the newly established offices of the Dutch *Militair Gezag*. His first letter to Marie refers to the abruptness of his departure.

> **September 17, 1944.** My *schatje*, I am writing my first dispatch sitting in a most luxurious bedroom of a first-class hotel. Brussels gives the appearance of a peaceful town being invaded by Allied columns. I am told it is only appearance. But what with packed cafés and dancings and well-dressed people it is difficult to feel war. We are repeatedly being told that this impression is false, and also that Holland is so much worse off. Since it is late, I want to make this short. Look after yourself and tell the little ones about their Papa. Try to let me know how they react. Thank Poelhekke for all his trouble. He was a brick. I feel guilty that I left him so abruptly. Give my

love to all, also at the office. My lovely *schatjes* whom I could not kiss goodbye receive this "God bless" from over the water. And you, *lief kindje,* in all I do, in all I experience, my thoughts are with you. I'll pray for my God-given lovely family. God bless you all.

Eindhoven, The Netherlands

Within days after arriving in Brussels, Jan is sent to Eindhoven, a Dutch town in an area bordering Belgium. The town has only just been liberated—on September 18, as a first step in the Allied forces' attempt to liberate all of Holland and advance into Germany.[58]

The southern province of Brabant, where Eindhoven is located, is separated from the northern Dutch provinces by the Rhine, the Meuse and their tributaries.* After freeing Eindhoven, the Allies planned to secure a series of bridges that would have allowed them to cross into the northern provinces. American, Canadian, and Polish troops participate in this largest airborne battle of World War II, known as Operation Market Garden—a battle that lasts from September 17 until September 24. To assist in this effort, on September 17, the Dutch government in London calls for a railroad strike in The Netherlands to hamper German transportation of supplies, troops, and weaponry.[59] Although the Allies succeed in capturing the first bridge

---

* The Dutch usually refer to this southern province as *Brabant,* as does Jan in his letters. The official name, however, is *Noord Brabant,* to distinguish it from the Belgian province with the same name.

at Nijmegen, they are unable to capture the final bridge at Arnhem.**

The failure of Operation Market Garden has a devastating and unexpected effect on the Dutch provinces still under German occupation. These areas north of the Rhine delta will suffer greatly from German *razzias*—round-ups of able-bodied Dutch men needed to replace and supplement the dwindling German labor force. Worse yet, following Operation Market Garden, in retaliation for the ongoing railroad strike, the Germans block all transport of food supplies from the agricultural eastern provinces to the urbanized west.[60]

Jan's describes his shock at the suffering around him.

> **September 23, 1944.** I hope this letter reaches you, and that I may soon hear from you. I don't know where to start. In a town without water, gas, or electricity I had to find accommodation for my party (one Canadian, one South Rhodesian, and the driver). Two days I have been without rations, sleeping in my bag. Thank God for my blanket! I have been moved to tears by the reception in this badly battered town.*** I almost cried when I saw

---

** The battle is commemorated in the 1997 film, *A Bridge Too Far,* directed by Richard Attenborough. The film is based on *The Classic History of the Greatest Battle of World War II* by Cornelius Ryan (New York: Simon and Shuster, 1974).

*** On September 19, the day after Eindhoven's liberation and the departure of the German troops, the Germans in an unexpected act of retaliation bomb the town while its citizens celebrate their first day of freedom. More than 200 civilians are killed, including 41 whose shelter takes a direct hit. Source: Margry, Karel. *De bevrijding van Eindhoven. The Liberation of Eindhoven* (Eindhoven: Drukkerij Lecturis) 114-115.

Map of The Netherlands in 1945.
The map identifies the main rivers and towns mentioned by Jan.

how the swines have drained the town from all what could be useful. I have passed on rations to a family who had not seen meat or cheese for two months. A man who rushed out of his house when news went round that there was a Hollander in that Allied car gave me a pre-war Dutch cigar. He had kept that one for the first countryman from overseas.

The town and country have been bled dry. Children begging for food. Old men coming out to ask for some tobacco. Cleaning squads pulling down dangerous walls. Gunfire at some distance, great activity overhead. That is the picture around me. I lunched on some bread and Spam and hot tea from my flask. I am soaked through. It has been a strange homecoming. I now understand what those people have been through these four years. The brother of a colleague told me how many a youngster under ten fainted in the class: underfed. Sorry *schatje*. I cannot write coherently. My thoughts are too fast for my pen.

I have set up a head office in a small hotel and received American and British reinforcement. Despite the difficulties and discomforts, despite getting soaked and being hungry, I should not have liked to miss this work for anything.

The American and British reinforcements to whom Jan refers in his letter are no doubt the American and British censors assigned by SHAEF to Holland. SHAEF's censorship staffing includes Allied liaison officers along with trained censors such as Jan from the liberated area. SHAEF has given responsibility for field censorship to the Army Group commanders.[61] In Jan's case, this is Britain's 21st Army Group under Brigadier G. Neville.

On September 25, he visits Nijmegen in the immediate aftermath of the allied defeat at nearby Arnhem. This is his first view of a battle zone. According to family lore, he accompanied the Red Cross workers who negotiated with the Germans for the treatment of Allied wounded.

> **September 25.** I have just returned from the front-line town of Nijmegen. I shall not describe to you Nijmegen. It was terrible. Bombing, shelling, etc. Along the road I saw cattle dead, I saw the rows of graves of our Allied boys. War is a beastly thing.

According to SHAEF guidelines, on arrival in a city or area, the liaison must immediately contact all news-disseminating agencies in the locality for which he is responsible. This means developing collegial relationships with the war correspondents, getting local press and radio to accept the SHAEF censorship guidelines, and reporting to a plethora of "higher ups" (to use one of Jan's favorite expressions). These include Pelt in London; the officials of the Dutch *Militair Gezag* stationed in Brussels; and Brigadier Neville, also stationed in Brussels.

Items that have to be cleared by SHAEF censors include information on troops of various nationalities taking part in actions;

casualties and troop strength, civil affairs; confirmation of enemy allegations, atrocities, and the like; as well as resistance and underground movements.[62] Jan is extremely concerned about the accuracy of press reports. In several letters, he expresses great anger at the thought that readers will consider descriptions of existing conditions as "propaganda." Undoubtedly, this concern for accuracy fuels his decision in the following months to visit each newly liberated area and make sure that the reports he censors are accurate.

The importance of the censorship requirements is made clear when a London colleague, now a war correspondent, publishes an article that leads to the identification of several resistance workers, who, as a result, are executed by the Germans. Jan's superiors had approved the article, but Jan nevertheless wishes he could have prevented its publication.

> **October 8.** This morning I said goodbye to K. He was broken hearted. So was I. There was nothing I could do for him. To be sent home, just when he seemed to have reached the zenith of journalistic success, was a catastrophe as few men could have gone through without weeping.

Many of Jan's activities come under the general heading of what he calls problem solving. For instance, one of his first successful endeavors is reported, not by Jan, but by Van den Broek, the chief of the former *Radio Oranje,* who has been given the task of public broadcasting in liberated Holland. During the war, resistance workers had built a radio sender at the Philips Electronics plant headquartered in Eindhoven. In his history of *Radio Oranje,* Van den Broek commends Jan for his support in getting the necessary permits to broadcast from Eindhoven.[63]

Periodic Meetings in Brussels

Jan's daily life in Eindhoven is far from comfortable, even though, unlike the civilian population, he has warm clothing, hot meals, and additional rations of cigarettes, tea, coffee, and chocolate—as well as transportation and mail through British military channels.* Fresh fruit, electricity, and hot water, however, are as unavailable to the military as to civilians. Fortunately for Jan, his work calls for frequent meetings with officials at the *Militair Gezag* in Brussels and occasional visits to Antwerp. In both cities, if one can afford it, it is possible to buy fresh food, including fruit.**

> **October 8 (continued).** I sent the mess a case of grapes from Brussels, which they sent through to two children's hospitals. The nuns who received them cried. In Belgium there's almost a glut of the most marvelous fruit. My work took me today into

---

* The 21st Army Group consists of the First U.S. and Second British Armies together with units of the First Canadian Army. It is through them that Jan receives his NAAFI rations and his meals in a military mess. (NAAFI, pronounced "naffy," stands for the Navy, Army, and Air Force Institute, the British World War II military catering organization.)

** Not all of Belgium, however, is as yet liberated. In mid-December 1944, the offensive, known as the Battle of the Bulge, lasts over a month. Ultimately the Germans do retreat, but not until January 1945 is all of Belgium free. Source: Martin Gilbert, *The Second World War. A Complete History* (New York, NY: Henry Holt and Company, 1989), 618-623.

Jan traveling to or from Eindhoven. Fall 1944

Antwerp, where life is quite normal. I had a cream ice, ate some beautiful peaches and bunches of grapes, and generally enjoyed for a short while the busy-ness of a great city. I should not mind being posted to Brussels or Antwerp, where so many things are obtainable, which one cannot even get in London, though life in those towns is disgustingly expensive. I hope to get Pelt to agree to an expenses allowance. Today, e.g., I had to give dinner to my driver, whom I could not invite into the mess, since he was a civilian. He had driven me through the dark evening and was of course even more tired than I felt.

October 17. I am back again in Brussels for one day, and I have had a bath. A bath filled with 10 inches of beautiful clear hot water. I had to tip the boy 20 francs to clean it.

October 24. Back again in Brussels! Private bathroom has no hot water and on my bed are no sheets. I shivered last night. The chambermaid is trying to get me a blanket.

Jan's travels are possible only because he's attached to the British Liberation Army. The relative riches of which he speaks in Belgium are not available to people living only a few hours away in Brabant. There is no transportation; the borders are closed.

Missing Marie and the Children

Jan finds it difficult to adjust to yet another separation from Marie, now pregnant with their fourth child. The baby is due in May. He is also concerned about the V-1 bombs that the Germans have been aiming at London starting in June—several of which l have hit the Wraysbury area.*

October 11. Tell me soon what arrangements you are making or have made about the new

---

* The "V" stands for *Vergeltungswaffe*, which means "vengeance weapon." These flying bombs make a very distinct sound just before the bomb falls and explodes. Because of their distinct buzzing sound, Londoners call them buzz bombs, flying bombs, or doodlebugs. A total of 9,251 V-1 bombs are launched against southern England from June 1944 to January 1945. Although only 2,419 make it to their intended targets, they kill more than 6,000 people. Source: Webb and Duncan, *Blitz over Britain*, op. cit., 185-186.
A number of bombs that don't make it to their London target hits surrounding towns and villages, including Wraysbury, shattering Jan and Marie's sense of safety. In fact, in June 1944, when Jan was still in Wraysbury, one of the first flying bombs struck the Bells of Ouseley, a riverside pub in nearby Windsor.

baby. Are you in the hands of Dr. H? For heaven's sake, look after yourself and don't take any risks. Take all the help you can get and eat well. I have no doubt that you can get all the necessary assistance from the people around you, especially now when I am away. There is lots I want to hear from you. About you and the little ones, about the garden and the people around you, about the way you follow the sad story of Holland's plight. I am slightly concerned about those doodlebugs coming down your way. Strange as it may seem, from a long distance these things appear much worse than when one is actually in the reception area.

October 17. When you write what Jantje is saying and you tell me that he is coming out with so many new phrases I feel quite sad that I should miss that. In a few months' time he will be such a big boy who will have to get used again to the idea of having a Papa, who is mad about the rascal. Somehow the picture of that little precious gift from God comes more clearly and more often to my mind than that of the two little girls. It may sound strange to you, but I often hear him calling you, or see him in his cot, sitting up, having waited for me. Of all the pictures I look at I cannot help liking most the one where he comes running in, his hands and suit full of mud.

Is my *schatje* jealous that I write so much about the children and say so little about you? *Liefje*, listen to me. I miss you. I miss you terribly but I try to suppress all such thoughts, since around me are men who have been away from home so much longer. I miss you when I want to pour out my worries and difficulties. I miss you when I feel lonely—and I am afraid that is often, even when in a crowd or in Brussels. I miss you of course when I go to bed. I miss you, oh, I could go on and on.

Newly Liberated Towns

As much as he misses his little family, it is clear that he is pleased that circumstances have brought him to Eindhoven and the opportunity to visit recently freed towns and villages.

> **October 22.** It is great to see the feeling of relief of the people in the towns just liberated. Never mind whether the town is nearly destroyed, precious things have gone. Thousands of times I have heard them say: "Thank God you have come. *We zijn weer vrij*. We are free again." My heart bled when I saw the terrible destruction of some small villages which had put out the flags on the rubble.
>
> Last week I was on the site of two of the largest missionary houses and seminaries of the country. The Germans, before they left this place, which they had occupied, set fire to every building. To prevent the

farms from saving anything at all, they mined these places too.

If ever anyone talks to me about propaganda when such stories are revealed I am going to have a fight. They have acted as beasts. In Nijmegen and in Eindhoven the bastards were out to destroy when they left. Young Nazi Germans have been throwing flames in the houses just for the fun of destroying things. There is hardly a horse left in these parts. The farmers were forced to drive their cattle and horses to the frontier with the departing troops.

The nearby towns of Breda and Tilburg are freed in late October, without any civilian casualties, by the First Polish Armored Division. Jan writes Marie about his visit to Breda and Tilburg (which is the hometown of Toos Hazebroek):

> **October 31.** I had the thrill of being one of the first Dutch officers to enter Breda, where the crowds were absolutely mad with delight. I even covered my uniform with my raincoat to try to escape the handshakes which people wanted to give. They were thanking me for having come, and I felt ashamed not to be a fighting man.
>
> I visited Toos Hazebroek's mother in Tilburg and gave her news of the children. She and the young daughter were so delighted. A bottle of wine and cigars were produced while I talked about Jan and Toos and the little ones. It was all moving to the

extreme. I promised to come back, which I shall try to do. I gave the family some tea from my stock.

The Germans have been up against it in Holland in a way which is marvelous to hear. My God, some people have been brave. Later I hope to tell you some of the stories. I will not write to you about their worst atrocities, but you must know that in the last days in Breda the bastards took even the wristwatches off the nuns in the schools.

The Vught Concentration Camp

This same letter describes Jan's worst experience: a visit to the recently vacated German transit and concentration camp in Vught.* *Kamp Vught* held more than 16,000 men and women captured in Belgium and The Netherlands. Of the many horrors that took place here, one was the punishment that a group of women received for standing up for another female prisoner. Seventy-four women were pushed into a cell room of barely 9 square meters for more than14 hours. Ten died. The camp was liberated in October 1944 by Canadian troops. The departing Germans left more than 400 bodies in the courtyard—those who had been executed that morning.[64] The arrival of the Canadians saved a remaining 600 prisoners from being executed that afternoon. Jan visits the camp shortly after its liberation.

---

* The Germans named the camp *Konzentrationslager Herzogenbush* because of its location near the Dutch town *'s Hertogenbosch.* It was the only official SS [*Schutzstaffel*] concentration camp in northwest Europe. The camp was partially evacuated by the Germans on September 7, 1944, and was liberated by the Canadians on October 26-27. Source: "Vught Concentration Camp." Jewish Virtual Library. A project of the American-Israeli Cooperative Enterprise. www.jewishvirtuallibrary.org

The recently liberated and vacated Vught concentration camp.
October 1944.*

October 31 (continued). To the war correspondents I leave the description of the terror camp at
Vught. I have been there and for the first time in
my life I have understood that one's blood can boil.
I should like to take the millions of people of Great
Britain and the U.S. over to this place where at one
time 16,000 of my compatriots were in the hands of
the lowest elements of the human race.

---

* Brigitte de Kok, spokesperson the Dutch *Nationaal Monument Kamp Vught* identifies the location as the interior courtyard of the *bunker,* the prison barracks that housed
primarily inmates condemned to death. Source: E-mail dated June 26, 2014.
brigitte.dekok@nmkampvught.nl

November 2. The horrors of the Vught concentration camp are often in my mind. The oven in which the bodies were burned and the urns in which the ashes were raked should remain a monument of the degeneration of this so-called civilized century.

I was in barracks which had not [yet] been cleaned and investigated—barracks which the inmates had to leave in a hurry. One book lay open on a page with an old photograph of the royal family. From the floor I picked up a little Catholic prayer book. In it was written the date on which this young lad had started to read his prayer book from beginning to end, and the date that he had started all over again. I hope they are able to send this souvenir to his parents or maybe to his wife or sweetheart. In the rubbish, I also picked up a letter, which started, *Lieve Paps* [dear Pop], giving details of his health and telling how pleased he had been to read that so and so were well. These letters, strewn all over the floor, are being collected and sent back to the nearest relations.

Eyewitness stories of how especially the Jews were transported are terrifying. Your heart would be wounded to hear a Red Cross worker telling how hundreds of Jewish children, poorly dressed, were driven into good vans for transport to the east.* I have seen the room, without any ventilation or light

---

* In June 1943, hundreds of Jewish children were sent from Vught to the Sobibor extermination camp in Poland. Source: Jewish Virtual Library, op. cit.

where more than 50 women were pressed together, till several had died. No propaganda has ever been able to tell the full story of our people's suffering

Jan's New Billet and Office

Jan's distress at what he sees during his visits throughout Brabant is barely offset by seeing the joy of people finally free of the German presence and oppression. He is all too aware of the ongoing hardship endured by the civilians. He tells Marie that at the moment the food position is worse than during the occupation. The lack of fuel affects everyone, civilians and military alike.

> **October 20.** If it is as cold and rainy as it is here I hope you have a lovely fire. We have no fire or heating whatsoever is this bally place. You should feel my feet just now... all the same I can stand it better than some others. After all this is nothing compared to what is still to come. I must say one of the best buys you ever made were these long woollen pants.

However, Jan appears to be overly optimistic about his ability to withstand the cold.

> **November 3.** I am, sitting all wrapped in, crippled with lumbago, fed up as never before, worried to death that I may be out of the running for some time just at a moment, when so much has to be done and I can only do so much. A great many things can happen in a day—yesterday I felt fine. This morning I could not

get up. This afternoon, I received electric treatment at the local Catholic hospital, where I can go back again tomorrow morning. I pray that it may help. Already I have upset our plans. It sounds so conceited to say so, but without me my team is fairly helpless. I had planned to move my headquarters to another town, and leave a regional quarter behind in charge of one of my officers. On top of that I have to move my billet. Not that I mind, since this so-called hotel, unheated and drafty, is getting on our nerves. If the worst comes to the worse I shall try to get private accommodations in a not so cold place. Please do not tell everybody about my misfortune. I feel rather self-conscious about it all! My great fear remains, that I might have to be sent home, as a physical failure.

Variously described as sciatica, lumbago, or rheumatism, Jan's back problems will continue to plague him. Fortunately, Jan soon moves to a billet with a local family, the Huysmans.

> **November 5.** I have just brought my cases to my new billet. I had met the father of this charming family in the first few days in this town, and he had said that if I ever wanted a room I could get one. Anxious to leave my present place because of the draft and cold, and also because of the fact that my room is just above my office, which means that one never leaves work, I went to him and asked him whether his promise still stood. It did. There are four children in the family, who were absolutely thrilled to pieces about having an officer billeted on

them. "You are coming to eat tonight? Oh you must come! Look at the lovely buttons on this coat! How does that gas mask work? And the steel helmet, much better than the Germans had." There was a fight to take the things to my bedroom.

November 6. I have had my first night in my new billet and I have been very comfortable indeed. We had a fire last night, and talked about a great many mutual acquaintances, both in Holland and England. I had a warm wine—drunk before going up. My bed is very comfortable. Running water, cold of course, but all the same, pleasant. The maid is doing my room. My washing is going out to the laundry. The children are noisy but perfectly charming.

When Jan first moves in, the family members are total strangers. In his initial letters he refers to Mrs. Huysmans as "the lady of the house." After the war, when Marie and the children join him in Holland, the friendship between the two families grows. To Jan and Marie's children, the lady of the house becomes *Tante Maria*. Even though Jan is eventually promoted to Major Van Houten, he will always be *de Kapitein* to the four Huysmans children: Carla, Marianne, Wim, and Rudy.*

Jan also succeeds in finding a new office—although not quite as comfortable as his new billet.

---

* It would have surprised Jan to learn that in 1996, his granddaughter Monique van Houten (Jantje's eldest daughter) marries Marianne Huysmans's son Jelle Groeneveld.

November 8. We have moved our office today. I went to see the place for the first time today. It is lovely! There are still one or two windows left, and the cardboard in. I am told to hold out for a week or two. Sure not all the broken windows have been boarded up, but if you get the necessary permits from somewhere, and if you find somebody who can give an order to have the windows put in, things may be quite alright. There is coal too. Not in the fire, but in a shed quite nearby. If somebody finds the right man who can give the necessary permit and someone to make the fire, the place can be heated too. At the moment the place is rather cold, but after all most people have an overcoat. It is of course uncomfortable for people with lumbago, but such people should be scrapped anyhow, or at least overhauled somewhere in the rear.

Jan de Hartog, visiting Eindhoven, presents an even bleaker picture of Jan's office.

Undated [Letter from Jan de Hartog to Marie]. About his work he'll have told you everything, I'm sure. The only thing that I'm able to add is a description of his office. It is very easily described as an office like any other office anywhere, apart from the fact that it has no windows, which makes it rather a polar institution. How he manages to do anything there but blow his hands and his nose alternately is beyond my comprehension.

The demands of work and the discomfort of an unheated office are, at times, somewhat offset by parties with local colleagues and the social life in Brussels.

November 10. Van den Broek's group is giving a party tomorrow night. I have not decided yet, whether I am going. It may be a nice change.

November 12. It was a grand evening. I may have been drinking too much. I may even have made a bit of a fool of myself, singing songs, etc., but *kindjelief,* something had to be done to break me away from the oppressing office worries and difficulties.

This is in short the story of our big do. Of course, you want to know what were the girls like. Well the British nurses were very good looking, the Dutch not so. All were good fun. I danced—if one might call it dancing on the sardine-packed little floor— mostly with a Dutch nurse from my hospital. The question "you are married aren't you?" was soon asked—they are all the same. I had to tell her who you were, nationality, age, etc., and also whether you would like us (all our gang) to invite nurses to go to dances. I maintained yes, of course. My nurse felt that if she were married, she would not like her husband to go out drinking and dancing with strange girls. Well, that was not quite what was happening.

Jan at a social event in Eindhoven.
Presumably the party organized by Henk van den Broek. November 11, 1944.

On his next trip to the Brussels headquarters of the *Militair Gezag*, Jan is delighted to find not only the welcome company of good friends and colleagues, but once again the luxury of heat and a hot bath.

> **November 25.** I am at present in the finest officers'
> club I have ever been to. Had a good lunch, light music
> in the background, a good drink, and am now sitting
> in the reading room, writing paper provided. What a
> treat after my billet-town! In one of the best hotels, I
> had a hot bath and a good general scrub-down. I have
> my car and driver with me, which is a tremendous treat.
>
> Last night I dined with Bogaert and Huizinga; we
> went to some small dancing place, where I had one

dance on a packed little floor. All very pleasant. Since my presence became known here I have been invited to tea by S., to dinner by Anderson [correspondent for the New York Times] and Cronkite.[65] I shall not be lonely the next few days.

Several Possible Job Changes

During this same visit to Brussels, Huizing offers Jan a position in the *Militair Gezag* in Brussels.

> **November 25 (continued).** Huizinga is trying to persuade me to leave censorship, and take control of news-distribution, which is in a state of chaos, or rather which has not yet been properly organized.
>
> After long and mature consideration I have decided not to accept this change. I have just built up my own organization, and now I should have to start building up a fresh and at this stage more difficult one. Although I have never been keen on censorship, I must say that I prefer to see the thing through to the end. Actually I prefer Holland to Brussels, since life here is so normal. One gets attached to field duties, however strenuous at times.

In early December, Jan is faced with another possible transfer. Gerbrandy considers sending Pelt to Brussels to take over news distribution from Huizinga. If Pelt moves to Brussels, Jan will be assigned to London.

December 2. Good morning, *liefje*, I have just heard—but this is very confidential for you and certainly not for anybody who has any connection with my office—that my appointment in Pelt's place has been decided upon by all the Gods concerned. I have not been informed officially yet. This is a pest. I don't want the job. I don't feel physically able to take on the responsibility and I don't expect my colleagues to play ball. I would, of course, be [promoted to] major then, which might please you, but does not interest me in the least. It is all very worrying.

Jan is called to a meeting with Van Heuven Goedhart, the Minister of Justice. The meeting is not about a transfer to London but to Brussels.

December 3. Van Heuven Goedhart announced that Pelt is not coming to Holland after all, since he has not got the confidence of Queen and Cabinet. Van Houten can do the job [in Brussels] and will have to take it on his shoulders. The General [Kruls] had been there the day before, and that had been their combined conclusion! I fought. I protested and left without accepting. Van Heuven Goedhart's parting remark was: "You'll hear more about it." I left in rather a depressed mood. Honestly, I cannot see how I can escape.[66]

Jan is quite pleased when, at the last moment, it is decided that Huizinga can stay on.

December 11. Huizinga's head has been saved as acting chief. I am glad. Honestly I am quite happy to stay out of it. Don't complain that I have so little ambition. I simply have not got it in this direction.*

St. Nicolas in Eindhoven

Early December brings some relief to Eindhoven residents. Not only have the British succeeded in bringing in additional food supplies, but families are also looking forward to the Dutch *Sinterklaas* (the feast of Saint Nicolas). On December 5, the Eve of the Saint's day, children put their shoes by the chimney hoping for some chocolates, oranges, or small toys. Dressed in typical bishop's garb, the Saint is said to ride across rooftops on a white horse distributing presents to those who have been good.

> **December 1.** The British have dumped sufficient food here to enable a gradual improvement to subsistence level for the whole population in this area. If it had not been for the difficulty of transport, the food position would have improved weeks ago. Transport remains the bottleneck, though the British have made now a sufficient number of cars available to allow a steady flow to the liberated areas. On the whole, the people have been most forbearing in the past difficult weeks. Quite a lot has been done unofficially. The hospitals, e.g., were provided with

---

* An organizational chart from the *Militair Gezag* indicates that Pelt is head of Section XI from September 8, 1944, to January 1, 1945, and Huizinga from January 1, 1945, to May 25, 1945.

medical provisions. In the hospital there has been bread for the weakest patients—that is to say, white bread.

Nearly everybody is smoking English cigarettes. How they get them I don't know, but the British soldier is most generous and likes sharing his tobacco and his smokes. A certain amount of black market dealing in army goods has also brought food to the market, but often to the least deserving.

On all the shops are notices: exchange here your coupon for coffee; buy your bar of chocolate here, etc. There is meat in the shops. The shops are crowded. The new rations, coffee for the first time, and also chocolate and some salt, have given the people new hope.

People are out buying things for St. Nicolas. At exorbitant prices, cheap toys and so-called luxury articles are available in some shops. In the way of shoes and dresses, nothing is to be got. It will be a very poor St. Nicolas to the children of Holland. No doubt the soldiers, who know about the custom, will do something for them. Already arrangements are afoot to do something for the children at Christmas. I hope to accumulate one or two things to take part in the share-out, should I be here.

December 5. In the pouring rain, a couple of hundred children are queuing up outside an office nearby to receive their presents. You should see those youngsters,

with their wretched torn and mended suits, often without coats, wearing shabby shoes, waiting for the great
moment when they receive a toy (a cheap Woolworth
one), some apples, and some sweets. Some of the military
have organized St. Nicolas parties, which were marvelous. In some towns the military commanders have
organized an extra food distribution.

Jan's letters don't mention that several V-I bombs hit the surrounding area including one that kills 20 civilians in Eindhoven on
December 14. However, the few snapshots that he brings home,
and that Marie places in the family photo album, include one of a
de-activated V-1 bomb.[67]

An unexploded V-1 bomb near Vught. Late 1944 *

* Brigitte de Kok, spokesperson for the *Dutch Nationaal Monument Kamp Vught*
checked with military experts who confirm that this is a V-1 bomb that would have
been deactivated by allied military. Source e-mail dated July 4, 2014. brigitte.dekok@
nmkampvught.nl

Short Visit to Wraysbury

In mid-December, Jan finally visits Marie and the children. At least one day is spent in London. One work-related activity is an interview with a reporter from the *Catholic Times* on conditions in Holland. The article is published in that paper's December 29 edition.

December 29, 1944 [Interview with Former Public Relations Officer in the Netherlands Government in London, now Chief Press Security Officer in Liberated Holland]. Having spent the past three months in his own country, Capt. Van Houten returned to London last week for a few days and left again for Holland at the weekend.

... "Imagine the plight of the people during the whole of the four years of occupation," said Capt. Van Houten. "Round up of hostages, deportations, arrests and internments were the order of the day. The people lived in an atmosphere of continual suspense and a knock on the door was a thing that brought terror." ... Even now I was told, the people instinctively tremble when they hear the summons of the doorbell. ... At Vught, Capt. Van Houten ... visited the concentration camp that had the reputation of being the worst in the country. He saw the three furnaces in which bodies were burnt, the dissection room where they were cut up like carcasses, to facilitate the incineration. ... Yet the grounds of the camp were laid out like those of a public garden. There were well-trimmed lawns, beautiful flowerbeds and pleasant railed-off walks. ... At one time this camp held 16,000 victims and before they left the Germans killed hundreds of them.

As much as Jan enjoys his visit home, he feels duty-bound to return to Holland to spend Christmas with his men. He leaves England on Christmas Eve.

Christmas and New Year's in Eindhoven

Immediately upon his return to Eindhoven, Jan writes Marie to explain why he didn't feel he could spend Christmas in Wraysbury with her and the children.

> **December 24.** Somehow I still feel that you cannot quite understand that I had to go today. When I walked the crowded streets today and when I saw people with their young children, I felt a pang of regret that I had not taken the chance to stay till Wednesday. Ninety percent of men would have done it. Am I not too conscientious? Maybe. I am here. Almost alone, certainly lonely. More than ever my thoughts are with my little family, with my *vrouwtje*, who needs me, and whom I need, with Treesje, who so much wanted her Papa to stay, with Coletteke, who could not understand why I was going, with my boy, whom I wanted to talk to me freely as he talks to you, which he no doubt would have done if I had played with him more.

Darling *vrouwtje*, I kiss you with the tenderness and love I kissed you on the night of our formal engagement, before we went together to Holy Communion, to ask God's blessing on our future. Tonight I shall pray firmly and fervently, that I may soon be reunited with you and my little ones.

The Christmas Eve street scene in Eindhoven makes Jan question his decision to leave Wraysbury.

December 24 (continued). Drunken soldiers are shouting profane songs into the peaceful night. Christmas Eve is almost desecrated by the behavior of small groups of men, who do not, cannot realize, what this evening means to the Catholic population of Brabant. The night is clear and the sky lit. A gentle frost makes it a pleasant winter night. There is no midnight Mass for the people. Curfew hours do not permit it. In the chapel of my church, midnight Mass will be said for military only. I have decided to go there, though I had promised the boys [Wim and Rudy Huysmans] that I should go with them at eight. I feel that I want to take this first chance to attend a midnight service.

Christmas day and the day after Jan spends with his unit at army headquarters, in a town outside of Eindhoven "closer to the front." Jan does not specify the location, but it was probably Helmond, where the British Second Army Headquarters set up camp in October.[68]

December 26. This is Holland at its most picturesque. Brilliant sunshine on a frost-covered land, children out skating on the canals and the little lakes which are spread all over Brabant. I drove some 50 kilometers this morning and enjoyed the landscapes as seldom before. One day you must see the country as it looked this morning. Christmas passed by quietly and pleasantly. I spent the day with my unit. I felt it my duty to be with my British and American friends, who had to spend their Christmas in my country. I did not regret it. P. [a British colleague] gave the toast to the King. I followed with "to those we have left behind." Our Scottish driver, with wife and children in Scotland, could not drink the toast with dry eyes. We stood almost still as if we wanted to have a few seconds exclusively to our beloved, before the toast was drunk. I shall treasure those moments.

A few days later, he tells Marie that life in Eindhoven has become more difficult for civilians and military alike: Eindhoven is out of coal.

December 28. All over the place people are burning part of their own houses to get some heating. I saw today flower trays outside windows and old kitchen chairs being broken up for fuel. Everybody is dreading the next few weeks, which may be icy. I seem to be able to stand things well, but I am very warmly dressed. You cannot have any idea of the depressed state of affairs out here. One can do nothing to help people. Let me stop my sorrowful story about my compatriots; you might get fed up reading about it.

December 29. Couldn't you come over and warm me a bit? It is perishingly cold at the office: the coal supply has disappeared. We are doing our best to get some more or even some wood. In the meantime, we are really shivering. As I said before, it is bad enough for us military, but terribly hard for our civilians who are badly fed, badly clothed and badly tempered.... I am going home early since I am frozen. My room, even though unheated, is warmer than the office.

In addition to the lack of fuel and clothing, many are worried about family members who have been deported to labor camps in Germany. There are also increasing concerns about the well-being of friends and family members north of the rivers. Resistance workers who manage to get through the German blockade, and government reports from London, make it clear that the population is suffering. However, there is no system in place for personal communications. Jan therefore does not know that two of his four brothers and a brother-in-law have been caught in *razzias* and are now in German labor camps. His younger brother Jac is one of 50,000 men between the ages of 17 and 40 taken prisoner during the infamous *razzias* in Rotterdam on November 11, 1944.[69] Transported by train to Germany, Jac spends the next seven months under deplorable conditions, working in locomotive factories in Hanover and Bremen.[70]

December 30. I had a delightful evening yester-day. Jan de Hartog arrived in the mess. I took him home to the Huysmans, where he entertained us (some friends were there too) till eleven o'clock. We laughed and laughed as we have not done for a long time. The Huysmans were delighted. Huysmans suggested immediately to invite about 30 friends one evening to hear De Hartog give a talk. After great persuasion on my part, Jan accepted and the literary evening has been fixed for Tuesday [New Year's Day]. Something to look forward to!

I am also looking forward to Tuesday afternoon. Our mess is inviting about 50 to 60 children to a tea, with buns and chocolate, etc., which we have saved. With one other officer-organizer, I have found a conjurer to entertain the crowd. My sec-retary and the Huysmans' daughter and a friend of hers will be there to do the serving. We are invit-ing the children of the families in which we are bil-leted, between the ages of five and twelve. I have booked for six (also children of the people, where I have been entertained). You see, quite an interesting program.

December 31. New Year's Eve. Happy New Year, *lief kindje,* or as we say in Dutch and much more to the point: *Zalig Nieuwjaar* [Blessed New Year]. I only realized just now that you will get this letter in the New Year. I am not going to enumerate all my wishes. You know them. Just one big wish: That our little family may be reunited for always when our second son is born.

I went to 8:30 Mass. The sermon this morning impressed me. We were asked to look back on the road of 1944 before we take the turning to the new road. We remembered the 13,000 men and women who in the last two years fell in this province of Brabant alone by the hand of the executioner. The figure, though I knew it, startled me. There was no coughing in church, when we remembered the patriots who gave their lives for their country, their homes and their faith. In England nobody can fathom the feelings of the people here. There is fear and depression just now. Fear about the war. Not about its outcome, but fear about the length of this terrible struggle, in which thousands and thousands of men will still have to give their lives. Fear also about the possible surprises which the Hun may spring upon the liberated frontier parts. There is no joy at present. A heavy hangover after the great jubilation for the regained freedom presses on the minds of the people. I am continually being asked questions upon questions about everything which has a bearing on this war. It is tiring, but somehow I feel that I have to talk to allay their fears.

There is dissatisfaction too. The government, the military administration, the military, the local authorities, all are being blamed for everything which goes wrong. Problems are piling up. There is a little more food, but there is no coal. There are tens of camps, packed with evacuees, and there is no transport to take them away to more humane surroundings. There are homes and hospitals and institutes in the frontline packed with people, half starved, ill, and filthy, and there are no doctors. There is no transport, no aid in general for those unfortunates. People want news from their dearest in other parts, and there is no means of communication.

They are free, but at a price.

At midnight on New Year's Eve, Jan and his friends not only toast the coming year, but, as Jan writes Marie: "We drank your health at midnight. I had great difficulty to keep that throb in my throat under manly control."

CHAPTER VII

WAITING FOR LIBERATION
January to May 1945

Jan and his colleagues had hoped to start 1945 with a party for the local children. However, the New Year starts off with a German bombing raid at the Eindhoven airport. This raid is part of a German attempt to keep the offensive of the Battle of the Bulge going by attacking Allied airfields.[71]

> **January 1, 1945.** Mass was put off due to Jerry's activities, which rather upset a number of people. Our children's party this afternoon may flop since the Punch and Judy team and the conjurer have let us know that they are not coming since our mess is too dangerously in the center of the place.

> **January 2.** We had the children's party yesterday afternoon. It was grand. They sang, they drank, they ate, and they enjoyed themselves thoroughly. Four-year-old little girls—one reminded me of Coletteke—climbed on the table to sing and quite enjoyed the applause.

Jan's Home Away from Home

Jan is feeling more and more at home with the Huysmans family. Even without heat, his room is warmer than the office. Moreover, the family, especially the children, feel safer when he's there.

> **January 3, 1945.** This room contains the warmth of the house somehow. All the windows at the office have been put in. But the place remains a refrigerator all the same.

> **January 5.** I had an invitation to play bridge tonight, but I had promised the family that I should stay in to "look after" the children. The two young boys did not want their parents to go out unless I was there as a complete safeguard against any disturbance. Thus, I'll stay in.

> **January 6.** Spent last night looking after the children. They were as excited as ours are when Mrs. Pelt comes to look after them. Times for going to bed had been formally fixed. I made myself very popular by giving the youngest 15 minutes extra. The last few minutes of this quarter of an hour were spent standing before the clock, following the hands.

By sheer coincidence, that same evening, Jan de Hartog sends a letter to Marie describing for her Jan's Eindhoven home. Marie must have been reassured by the letter describing Jan's life with the Huysmans.

January 6 [Letter from Jan de Hartog to Marie].
The house where he is billeted belongs, as you'll
know, to an Eindhoven banker, with whose family
I spent two evenings after having been introduced
to them by your husband. The night I was there the
main thing that struck me was how your husband
has been made a "member of the family," and a
rather important one at that. The children simply
adore him and ascribe to him all sorts of military
genius and foresight. As long as he is in the house,
they seem to consider themselves somehow in safety,
which somehow gives a little idea of the state of fear
and apprehension which the people over there are
still living with—the possibility of a German break-
through constantly hanging over their heads. In
this general atmosphere of fear and rumors your
husband does very good work indeed, mainly by
being what he is. You know how we appreciated
him already here in London. His integrity and
sublime common sense were, somehow, a tonic.
Now, in liberated Holland, these qualities prove
even more precious. To see him sitting in the family
circle of this solid clan, laughing and reassuring ...
is a heartening picture indeed.

Increased Concerns about the Northern Provinces

January and February 1945 are periods of waiting—waiting for
relief from the cold, waiting for alleviation of the famine in the
northern cities, and above all, waiting for liberation of the entire
country. For Jan, a pervasive concern is the lack of specific news

about his family in Rotterdam. On the rare occasions that he gets news from someone who has escaped from the north, the news tends to be out of date.

Most Eindhoven residents have similar worries. Jan indicates that the occasional relaxing evenings playing bridge are offset by too many evenings spent answering questions about the progress of the war—questions to which he has no real answers but that people ask because he is viewed as a person with authority and government connections.

> **January 4.** I spent the evening with [friends] where I met a young man who has been in hiding these last nine months and was a personal friend of my youngest brother Nico. A year ago it seems Nico was put on a train to Germany for forced labor. For some reason the train could not leave the country. He was able to return home, where he managed to get a medical certificate that he was unfit. He—the visitor—did not know a great deal about the rest of the family, apart from the fact that the bomb damage to the houses opposite the old home, and in their own house, had caused quite a stir.*

---

* While still in England, Jan had learned about the 1942 bomb damage to his parents' home in the Claes de Vrieselaan. As a result, his parents and two youngest brothers are now living in a flat in the mostly unscathed Blijdorp section of Rotterdam. The bomb damage to the home of Jan's parents was confirmed by Hélène Boyen, a friend of Jan's niece Thea Holterhues-van Houten. Hélène checked the dates in the *Gemeentearchief Rotterdam* (the Archives of the city of Rotterdam) and learned that this bombing occurred on January 28, 1942. Source: Hélène Boyen, e-mail communications. October 24, 2009, and January 22, 2010.

Far from being pleasant, the evening became a bore and a drag, as a result of the criticizing questions, which I had to answer. People have become grumblers. I maintain that fear causes all the irritations. It may be that too many psychological faults are being made by the Military Administration, although I cannot see that. One really gets the uncomfortable feeling that people have become impatient about the progress of the war and blame this on any military they have a chance to meet.

To help people I have accepted a number of invitations to answer questions. Saturday afternoon I am meeting the editorial staff of a communist weekly, a most troublesome paper. In the evening I am meeting a number of journalists and industrialists in a nearby town. All this is no joy ride.

January 8. The population in very depressed in this miserable weather and the news is not helping them a great deal either. Today I saw a great lot of news from north of the rivers. It is appalling. Deportations go on wholesale. You will probably get the terrible story of the burning of 100 houses in a small village. This war and occupation is a most frightful thing. One cannot get hardened to it. At least I cannot.

Jan's reference to the burning of 100 dwellings in a small village undoubtedly refers to the German's retaliation against the killing of a German officer during an ambush by resistance workers in the small town of Putten. The Germans reprisal was swift. They forced people from their homes, separated the men and the women, burned over 100 houses, and transported most of the adult male population (more than 600 men) to concentration camps in Germany. Fewer than 50 returned.[72]

Visits to Brussels

The periodic trips to the offices of the *Militair Gezag* in Brussels continue to provide a stark contrast to conditions in Eindhoven.

> **January 11.** *Mijn lief vrouwtje*, this is a red-letter day. I had a hot bath. When I say hot, I mean hot. I had to add five inches of cold, to stand it. In the meantime I had to dance about to keep warm. I was in my bath half an hour after reaching town. Our journey was tiring on the slippery roads, but the scenery especially in the wooded parts was delightful. It is rather a shame that sitting cramped in a car, caused my latent lumbago or whatever it is, to become more active. I shall try to pack myself in well and be careful. Luckily I had taken my sleeping bag along—there are no heavy blankets on the bed of this first class officers' hotel.

> **January 12.** Crowds, well-stocked shops, cinemas, theatres, clubs, and still lonely. This town does not give one rest. One has to do things. We— five officers—went to two so-called nightclubs, and talked shop. The first was the best-decorated, stylish first-rate club I have ever been too. I should have

liked to have been in a mixed party, just to have a dance. The second place was noisy, loud too in its makeup. Both were expensive and really boring for the non-dancers.

Bogaert left [for London] this morning, before I had time to buy something for the children. Hard luck. I walked through the streets and gave my eyes a treat of good looking, well-dressed, and well-groomed women. Played with the desire to take one to a theatre or a dance, but as always it remains a play of thoughts. Somehow I understand that so many men pick up someone from somewhere to go out with. To be always with men, none of whom you can call a friend, gets your goat. I am off again tomorrow, if I can get transport. I shall be glad. This is a nice break and as such quite pleasant. Kisses to my little ones. Tell them that I shall buy them some toy, if you write that they deserve it!

Later that day. It is about nine. I have just had my dinner, on my own; I went to a newsreel at seven, on my own. I am going for a stroll now, on my own. I am not complaining. Just explaining why I am so happy to leave again tomorrow, out of the warmth of this luxury place to the cold dullness of my forward "home."

I did not buy anything but some nougat and expensive chocolates. This is an amazing town. Many are too poor to buy any of these expensive sweets and goods generally. I saw, just as in Holland, women scraping the bits of coal out of the gutter where a coal van had unloaded. All the same it is not so cold here as up north. Let these few lines serve as proof that my thoughts are with you, if proof should be needed, which I doubt. I walk through toyshops to be able to picture the reaction of my children should they see what I can. I look at everything with you standing next to me, and I try to guess what you would think and say.

Eindhoven

Back in Eindhoven, Jan finds himself once again being the unwitting the spokesperson for the *Militair Gezag*.

January 17. I cannot help telling you a little about the atmosphere in which we are trying to do our work. One can do so much to give people moral encouragement when they are caught in spasmodic fits of depression. The strange thing is that very often an evening talking about all sorts of problems, to which I hardly know the answers, helps to create a better feeling.

I played bridge last night [with friends of the Huysmans]. It was all very pleasant and relaxing. Excellent wine enhanced the feeling of being out of the rut. I had brought along a pocketful of your tea, for which I have to pass on to you well meant thanks. They are a charming family. Happy despite their tremendous worries. Six months ago, their eldest son, a student, was in hiding in Amsterdam. They haven't heard a word since. The boy had suffered from his lungs many years ago and they fear with great fear.

Behind the façade of happiness of being free at last, there lies a mountain of worry and fear in nearly every home in this town. Concern about their nearest relatives in battered northern Limburg and in bleeding Holland north of the rivers.

A young man reached freedom yesterday who was in The Hague quite recently. I spare you his description of the misery there. Not so much the misery of hunger, of threatening starvation and destitution, but of the ever-present fear of the *razzias*. Many of the men and boys who are driven out of their houses for deportation to Germany or for forced labor or some defense site are sent there on freight trains.

There is one thing which keeps people going. The certainty that they too will be free "soon." What amazes me is that there are still secret papers being distributed giving the news from London. National distribution has become impossible. Right now every town, every district prepares its own clandestine newssheet. I take off my hat to those journalists and printers, who are risking their lives every hour of their days and nights.

January 21. My quiet evening last night was rather upset by the arrival of David Anderson [from the New York Times], who wanted copy for an article.

As it happens I had ample material and I was able to provide him with a first-class story from occupied Holland. It is not my job at all, but since I am the only one forward, I simply have to step in. Although my own work gives me more than sufficient to do, I am forced—in the absence of others—to do a deuce of a lot more.

Tonight I am addressing a private meeting of ten former illegal [resistance] workers, who have a lot of criticisms and who want to put questions to someone. During the last four months I have hardly had a Sunday to call my own. Today again I received two requests to come and talk to a little meeting of people. It is always the same sort of question about the government, the military administration, about Gerbrandy and the Catholics, etc.

January 24. I cannot refrain from mentioning my tremendous concern over the chaotic and famine conditions in occupied Holland. The latest news is simply terrifying. God give there may be some help soon. One feels ashamed ever to grumble, when one reads about the terrible plight in Holland's main cities. Let us thank God that we are so fortunate to give our little ones all they need, that they are not amongst the tens of thousands starving infants in the homes of my country. I tremble when I think of the horror for fathers and mothers, who see their children suffer. We have every reason to be grateful.

The next day, Jan visits some recently liberated villages. He does not specify the location, but the villages may have been in the Dutch province of Limburg, which is only partially liberated. It won't be fully free until March.

January 25. It was a more than dreadful sight. Not a house stood upright, not twenty houses of a large village can possibly be recovered and made habitable. Most of the people had been evacuated; the loss of life has, thank God, been comparatively small. On a few of the ruins the red, white, and blue flag flew defiantly. From the gaps in walls where once windows were, I saw some festive orange-colored balloons.

The next place, from where the Germans had been shot out only a few days ago, was partly intact. Many inhabitants had returned. Others were seeking their few possessions. On the roads were women with young children in blankets trying to find shelter, fleeing from neighboring villages which were still under fire. Only the main roads had been cleared of mines.

Along the roads burnt-out tanks, German and Allied. Small wooden crosses paid honor to the lives of the men who fought for my country. There were no cheers, only anxious inquiries: Is that place free? How can I get news from my son who has been deported? The scene was heart-rending. One could do nothing. Just feel sorry and bitter. Sorry for those families and their homes. Bitter about the destruction by the Germans, who are out to destroy all.

[Civil] Affairs are dealing with thousands of people who are ill, even dying. Back in my warm hotel— no hot water though—I can hardly appreciate the comfort. I have to think of the misery I saw today.

A Possible Transfer to London

In mid-February, Pelt presents Jan with an interesting proposal.

February 13. Pelt has proposed to the Chief of Staff to detach me to the London office for some time, in fact till the possibility of an Allied crossing over the rivers. He wants me to take up my old post, to push the Dutch propaganda abroad, which has been failing a bit. Well, that was not my idea at all of my coming to London for a while. I don't want to stay there for a lengthy time. There is so much to be done here! And I hate to take somebody else's place in London. I am really in an amazingly difficult position. I should love to be in London for some time. Pelt and Gerbrandy want me to be in London for quite a while. Faced with this marvelous opportunity to see you, I hesitate. *Partir, c'est mourir un peu.* I belong here, with the people whom I can help such a lot. But I won't oppose Pelt's plan since it gives me the marvelous chance to be with you and the children for a while. If the Chief of Staff agrees, you can expect me next week.

However, a little over a week later, it is with a heavy heart that he tells Marie that the London posting won't happen.

February 24. A message has just come in from Pelt. General Kruls is opposed to Captain van Houten leaving Holland for London. On Wednesday Pelt will come and explain. It breaks my heart. I understand how you feel. Sorry, darling. I cannot write any more just for the moment. Just received your letter. It makes me weep to read that the children are so sure that I shall be coming home. Tell them that I am very busy, and that I am very very sorry that I cannot come.

To Marie's surprise, Jan arrives in Wraysbury on March 1 for a weeklong visit. Then, back in Eindhoven, he writes that it may be a while before he can send any letters.

March 13. Some important work has cropped up the morning. Don't be disappointed, don't worry and don't expect to get a letter every day. I shall be traveling about a great deal and may not have an opportunity to write.

Queen Wilhelmina Visits the Liberated Provinces

What Jan cannot yet tell Marie, for censorship reasons, is that Queen Wilhelmina will be visiting Zeeland, Brabant, and Limburg, the three provinces, south of the rivers. To ensure her safety, preparations are made in deepest secrecy. Planning is done in conjunction with the Allied forces and with Prince Bernard, now living and working in Breda, west of Eindhoven. It is Jan's responsibility to ensure that the Queen's visit will not be announced in the press or on the radio.

To Jan's surprise, Prince Bernard and Pelt have arranged for him to be the Public Relations Officer for the press party. Thus, he accompanies the Queen on her historic visit.

On March 13, the Queen crosses from Belgium into Zeeland for her 10-day visit. In a diary, which Jan cannot send to Marie until after the Queen has safely returned to London, he records his observations and reactions. He entitles his narrative "Royal Trip through Liberated Holland" and prefaces it with a note to the British censors. "In this personal report of Queen Wilhelmina's journey through liberated Holland, I am complying fully with all censorship press instructions." The note is signed J.A. van Houten, Chief Press Censor for Holland.

> **March 13 (continued).** It was a lovely homecoming. No bands, not much brass, just ordinary people welcoming their Queen. Pale from emotion, the Queen walked over the white line and stood there for a while looking around. The national anthem was sung; we stood to attention. She shook hands with a great many of the farmers, women, and children. They told her their story, and she listened politely and asked questions. She listened and asked questions all the way. Once I, too, had to blow my nose when she stood talking to a little boy and girl, the only survivors of a large family. The kids were crying and stood there, sobbing in front of their Queen. The situation on this corner of Zeeland defies description.
>
> **March 14.** Crowds lined the street from early morning. Word had been passed around the night before

that the Queen would be visiting Axel, Hulst, and Terneuzen. One moment stands out particularly clearly in my mind. Just over the canal at Terneuzen our procession halted. The Queen was introduced to a naval man, arm in a sling, pale, insignificant looking. The only survivor of six heroes in this town, he took her a hundred yards along the riverbank to a spot where the other five had been executed. On the slab of stone, amidst a mess of wire and rubble, she laid down a rosette of red, white, and blue. These men had removed explosives which the Germans had put underneath the bridges and sluices of the canal. Facing the bridge, they had been liquidated.

The tour went on. We stopped along the roadside to inspect troops, to have a few words with small groups of farmers. The procession stopped at all the market squares, where the crowds went mad with delight. It was a relief today to visit places, which were intact.

On March 15, the Queen visits the island of Walcheren, which in November 1944 had been flooded by the RAF to rout the Germans.[73]

March 15. Miles of flooded country. Devastation everywhere. West Kapelle, where the dike was breached, where the village had to suffer the horrible, but under the circumstances, necessary fate of destruction, provided the clinch of this dramatic tour. Completely isolated, reachable only by amphibious "duck" passing the edges of the dunes, against which the carcasses were still lying of the many horses and cows which had fled to high ground only to be killed by land mines. Probably a few hundred women and children received their Queen amongst these ruins which they have refused to leave. They grouped around her when she stood, far forward in the mud, staring at the gap in the dike through which the sea poured its waves.

It struck us all how beautiful, how full of character, the faces of these people were. They waved to us from their top window while the waves belched through the rooms and doors below. Those doors. I'll hear that sound for many years to come. One wave pushes them open and then that water bangs them back. Only here and there locks had withstood the water.

March 16. The first really official session took place this morning in Middelburg. The Queen delivered her first address. I felt annoyed at the presence of a woman with four young children who were difficult to keep silent in this solemn place. During the one-minute silence, the cry of the baby in arms gave the proceedings a strange character. We were remembering the dead, and as I later understood, also the father of these four youngsters who was executed in September last for sabotage. The cry of this baby: I shall remember that too as long as I live. With shame, I think back at my irritation about the presence of these children.

Had the best dinner for years. One of our party treated us to oysters. Heaven knows how many. Drink flowed generously. This morning we are having a rest. The town has its normal appearance. The secret of the important visitor has been maintained. Not a word has been leaked.

After visiting Tilburg and Breda, the Queen reaches Eindhoven on Sunday, March 18. Jan writes of the excitement and exultation he sees.

March 18. The town gave her Queen a rousing reception. Thousands lined the road where the thickest crowd ever had been waiting for hours. Hardly had the Queen's car stopped when the crowds broke the cordons of police. A narrow path remained clear. Carla Huysmans offered a bunch of flowers, the crowd cheered and sang, women wiped away tears.

In Eindhoven he learns that the secrecy of the Queen's visit has been broached:

I soon forgot about the delightful scene. Two of my staff informed me that one of the newspapers had jumped the release and announced the Queen's visit in today's edition. Since then I have been doing nothing but make arrangements for this leak not to spread, and have forbidden this newspaper to be published for the next seven days. Monday brings even worse news. The BBC broke the news blackout at 7 this morning. It caused a hell of turmoil. All day I had to make phone calls and travel to try and find a solution for this unexpected news mishap. It upsets all my censorship arrangements. At 6 in the evening, I had a compromise-solution accepted by 21st Army Headquarters and by Prince Bernard.

From Eindhoven, the trip continues south to Limburg, where the Queen visits Maastricht, Venlo, Roermond, and Heerlen. Here Jan's peace of mind is totally destroyed by the frantic reports from Eindhoven that some more censorship breaks have occurred in London.

> **March 22.** Honestly, I cannot see how I can get out of this mess, which has developed fully outside my control. As far as I can see, the press and radio under my control have made only one minor mistake. It is really heart-wrenching to feel that after all the trouble I have taken things have gone so completely wrong from the purely censorship point of view. I fear it is a nasty smear on my reputation. Thank God, we have managed to keep the general security in hand.

The tour ends in Venlo, where Prince Bernard is waiting at a nearby airport from where the Queen flies back to London.[74] Jan and his colleagues travel on to Brussels. He is now free to release information the news media about the Queen's visit.

> **March 23.** At 8, I joined my British and Canadian friends, who had invited me to dinner. It was good but too beery. At 11, I sailed home on my own. I wanted to be in before midnight. It has gone midnight now.

What shall I say about our final days? Talk about the total destruction of Venlo and Roermond? About the sick and disabled who were lying in front of the town hall in Venlo to see their Queen? About my being introduced to the Queen and my introducing her to four of our war correspondents? It is too late at night to reflect back on these memorable ten days. I'll tell you about it, if and when I can come home.

A Holiday in Wraysbury

Jan returns to England a few days later and spends from March 26 to April 9 with Marie and the children. Marie is now eight months pregnant. He is happy to know that even if he cannot be there when the baby is born that Mrs. Pelt has offered to stay with Colette and Jantje when Marie is in the nursing home with the new baby. Treesje will stay with friends in the village.

Back in Eindhoven, he wishes Marie an early happy 31st birthday and an easy delivery.

> **April 11.** Should this letter arrive near your birth-day, I want you then to consider this my "many happy returns" and "wishes." It is difficult to phrase wishes for you know as well as I do what I have utmost in my mind, but here goes:
>
> A fine healthy boy who behaves, and gets into the right position.

A comparatively easy time at birth and the
best comfort possible in the nursing home.

A very early opportunity to parade through
the village with your daughters and sons,
and a figure which makes people say: you'll
never believe she has four children!

Lastly, an early return of your husband—even if it
must be a short stay—to tell you: thank you darling
vrouwtje for our second son, or for our little daughter;
thank you for all you have gone through again. To tell
you also that he is very proud of his family—I begin
to drop the "little"—and still very much in love.

Liberation of the Eastern Provinces

In early April, the Allied forces once again attack the German
defenses around Arnhem. This time they succeed. Arnhem is liberated on April 14; the Allies can now follow a northeastern path
into Germany.[75] The eastern provinces are free. Jan tells Marie that
as soon as possible he hopes to visit the newly liberated areas and
see his sister Loek and her family in Deventer.

On April 15, which happens to be Marie's birthday, Jan is reunited
with his sister and her family.

> **April 16.** In the late afternoon of your birthday,
> I walked up Loek's stairs, having pushed the door
> open myself and was received by [her husband]
> Martien [Venselaar], who was too flabbergasted to

say anything at all. I entered the small room where Loek was feeding her three little ones. Loek paled and burst into a torrent of tears. I was rather moved too. She looked old and thin and worried. They have been managing, but were worried to death about Rotterdam. Loek was delighted when I unpacked my tea, chocolate, soap (!), and quite a lot of other most welcome luxuries. We talked and looked at snaps which included a number of spare ones. My good mother is unrecognizably thin, and that was half a year ago. They have been sending food parcels to Rotterdam but little arrived: all stolen.

Loek has had a terrible time. In October she had to go to hospital for a miscarriage, while the children had whooping cough and had to be looked after by Martien. He did not dare leave the house to see Loek in view of the *razzias* and the fear of being caught. For weeks they lived in the cellar, as they did again in the days before liberation when there were heavy bombardments. The town is fairly heavily damaged, but Loek and her little ones have escaped all harm. The children are healthy, though very pale having lived indoors for so long.

The family spent so many nights in the cellar that they and their neighbors constructed doorways between their houses so that the adults could visit during the long evenings while the children slept.[76] The most recent bombardments were the result of American error. In February, American bombers attacked several Dutch towns, including Deventer, Arnhem, and Nijmegen, believing them to be in Germany.[77]

April 16 (continued). Today going north, I came across a heart-rending scene. We had to stop near a ferry. An old man and a young man spoke to me: they were pushing a heavily laden bicycle without tires. They wanted to get to Rotterdam. I told them you cannot, you cannot cross through the Allied lines to German-occupied territory. "But we must, my wife and children are starving, we have cycled 80 miles to here to get food. Before we found food, the Germans took away our bicycles and left us along the road. Somebody gave us this frame, and we want to push it to Rotterdam. We have a bag full of potatoes and other food."... The shadow of Rotterdam and starvation.

Thousands and thousands of children lined our route in this flat agricultural country. Most of them were evacuees from western Holland. The churches combined have gotten them there. Friesland's capital, packed with evacuees from Limburg, today celebrated its liberation. There were cheers all day. I was sort of mobbed as the first Dutch officer they have seen. I really could write for hours about this unforgettable sunny journey through the orange, red, white, and blue-decorated towns and villages of Holland's northern provinces.

I shall not spoil the happy picture and delightful harmony by saying too much about the heartbreak stories one comes across. Tonight I'll say an extra little prayer to thank God that he has spared our home the suffering which so many had to endure. Just a picture: a lady standing outside her house waving to the troops. The red, white, and blue is proudly flying from the top windows. Says our local guide: her three sons were shot just a week ago for resistance work.

The evacuees from Roermond and Venlo ask us about their towns, and we have to admit what they already know, from rumors and reports, that both towns have been completely destroyed.

The curfew was put at 9, but at 10 large groups of young folk were still parading the streets and squares, and singing patriotic and British songs. They are mad with delight. The Tommies are having a heavy time in fraternizing. (I am missing many a treat!) Good night, *schat*, my eyes are sore with this candlelight.

April 17. I have had a quieter day. More wanton Hun destruction, more cheers, more flags when one more town becomes free, more sunshine, and more beautiful scenes of Holland's picturesque country with its large lakes, well-kept farms, and stylish homes. Chance took us to a British mess where we were well looked after. Your candles have come in very useful.

Already the refugees and evacuees are trying to get to their homes in the west and the south, though movement is impossible. Nearly every farm harbors children from the west. This is the best dairy country in the world and all the children look fine and healthy. I've had some milk and eggs today!

April 18. I am sitting in a small room in a little town far away from all industrial life. We have found a billet. Once more, thank God for my sleeping kit! I have just made an arrangement with a woman to cook our food. Her two children with leaking noses are entertaining us.

Having driven a further 20 miles in a car with the sunroof open, I am quite sun-tanned. Driving every day a deuce of a number of miles is tiring. Needless to say, almost every day is cramped with experiences, fine ones but also terrifying ones. The sight of those boys and young men tramping back from Germany and from places on Holland's eastern frontier towards "home," dragging along their few possessions, is heartbreaking. Today we have not seen much destruction. These parts have been spared the ravages of war, though the story of the forced deportation of men is general.

April 21. In my short scribbles during my five-day journey in the newly liberated parts, I have already given you a fair day-to-day picture of my experiences. You have understood these have been very mixed. The last day put a depressing finish to it: the sight of Arnhem. This beautiful Dutch city has been completely destroyed. I saw two persons

only among the rubble of what was once a flour-
ishing well-to-do town, à la The Hague. It seems
that nearly everybody has been evacuated from this
area.*

But all this is nothing compared with the slow
assassination of people in the west. *Kindjelief,* I
shall not depress you, but I must share with you
the feeling of horror of what is going on in the
big towns of western Holland. The photos which
have come through of the children and old dying
in Amsterdam of sheer starvation are indescribable. If these four million people are not going to
be liberated in the next 10 days, there is going to
be a disaster, as western Europe has never known.
At present the number of deaths through starvation
remains comparatively restricted, but in a few weeks
time, tens of thousands are due to succumb. In the
south, there is depression all around. People are full
of fear and anxiety for the people in the west. There
is an almost revolutionary spirit: give us arms, and
we fight our way to our people. I know that we can
do nothing, and have to rely on our Allied friends.
God give that Eisenhower may decide that the early
liberation of western Holland, though strategically
not necessary, has become a moral responsibility.

---

* In October 1944, following Operation Market Garden, the Germans ordered the
evacuation of close to 100,000 civilians from Arnhem. Those who tried to return found
the city cordoned off by German patrolmen. Source: Van der Zee, *The Hunger Winter.*
Occupied Holland 1994-1945 (Lincoln, Nebraska: The University of Nebraska Press,
1982), 46-47.

April 22. You must not count on my coming home when the baby is born, though I shall put in a great effort to get a few days' leave as soon as you are home again. I wish I knew how you could let me know how you are by telephone or wire. There must be a way. Mrs. H. at the office might be able to lay on something, either through ANEP or through Mrs. Van den Broek of *Radio Oranje*. She might know a way open for such an urgent message. Look after yourself, and good luck. If it is a son, I'll give him a thousand kisses, a daughter 999. It is up to you.

Famine in the Western Provinces

The food shortage in the western cities is partially alleviated in February when the Germans reluctantly allowed the neutral Swedes and the Swiss to bring in barges with flour, cod liver oil, and medications.[78] However, it is not enough to feed the population. By late April, the food shortage is so acute that the Germans agree to let British bombers make food drops. These drops start on April 28 and last for 10 days. Seven thousand tons of food are dropped over western Holland in what becomes known as Operation Manna.[79]

April 25. The announcement this morning that the British are going to drop food over western Holland gave us here the feeling of relief, so necessary to do our work well. Ten days there has been a feeling of extreme depression. Nobody talked without bringing up the subject of famine in western Holland. It was becoming a haunting picture, affecting everybody's life. May everybody get a share of this precious food.

April 28. *Radio Oranje* gave us tonight the exciting news: food will be sent and efficiently distributed. Germany is cracking. We should celebrate! The news today has been so overpowering, so tremendous, that I can hardly digest it all. I am sure you are following things as closely as I am, and I often think of you listening to the news, which apart from everything else may mean so much for the reunion of our little family.

May 2. Once again my thoughts have been wandering over to Wraysbury and our little home. I should be there. Right now. The show here is practically over. Thank God for that. I have never been so impatient. Around us we witness great Red Cross activity. I hate to be doomed to comparative inactivity at the moment. Somehow I feel there is so much more important work to be done than has been assigned to me for the present. But let me not complain to you.

I want to talk about our little home, about you and the children. Having had time to re-read your latest batch of letters, I could not suppress a feeling of longing to get home, to leave everything behind and settle again in my little village. I ought to be with you, help you to make all arrangements. Help you to look after the little ones, be with you on the day of the birth of our new son or daughter. I want to be near you. This is ridiculous.

Tomorrow or the day after, I may have to start traveling and miss all your letters for quite a time. Even the announcement of the baby's birth may reach me with considerable delay. The great urge to see my people as soon as possible has subdued. I know now that they are going to be fed. I don't mind at all if I am going to see them some time after the liberation, if only I could be sure that I could be with you for a little while after your confinement.

Liberation

On May 4, 1945, the British senior military commander, Field Marshall Bernard Montgomery, accepts the surrender of the German troops in northwestern Europe.[80]

> **May 4, 1945.** Treesje's birthday. At 8:30 the news came through. We went delirious with delirious with delight. Never in my life shall I forget those moments between 8:45 and 9:00 in the evening on the 4th May 1945. Flags were hoisted all around. I have never before seen such a sight. Even fireworks had been prepared! Holland is free. The great dreaded disaster has been prevented. God give that I may find all my people in reasonable health. My son or daughter will be born in peace. In a crowded

room of people I hardly knew, I have toasted you
and the baby, who will be a peace baby.

May 5 [in the early hours of the morning]. The
excitement last night was indescribable. For nothing
in the world would I have wanted to miss the sight
of the red, white, and blue being hoisted all over
town, while, within a few minutes of the announcement, the bells started tolling. People embraced one
another. The young folk danced in the street. For
the first time in five years, the street lamps went on.

CHAPTER VIII

THE WAR'S AFTERMATH
May to December 1945

Although officially the Germans have surrendered, Johannes Blaskowitz—the commander-in-chief of the German army in The Netherlands—does not at first acknowledge that this surrender applies to western Holland.[81] Not until the afternoon of May 5 does Blaskowitz agree to meet in Wageningen with Canadian Commander General Charles Foulkes. They meet, but the capitulation does not get signed that day. Blaskowitz requests 24 hours to review the terms of the surrender—during which time he agrees to halt the hostilities.[82]

Jan experiences this refusal to surrender when, on the morning of May 5, he attempts to drive to The Hague. The next day, he happens to be in Wageningen when the capitulation documents are signed.

> **May 6 [In the morning].** Back home again! Where shall I begin? I left for the West yesterday morning. Packed and full of confidence that I could arrive straight into The Hague. That was

not to be. We drove up to the gun emplacement on the front line. For the troops there was no armistice yet. The other side was still firing, and one Dutch car, which wanted to drive straight through to The Hague, was shot up on what was understood to be a mine-clear road. We had to return to Eindhoven.

May 6 [In the evening]. Today, by sheer luck, we were in Wageningen when the conference took place between the British and the Germans about the armistice and the way the Germans were going to be disarmed and driven to prison camps. Although I could not get into the conference room, I could see the procedure and follow the conversations word for word in the BBC van, which was taking the whole down on records.

It was a thrilling experience. On one side of the road were the German drivers waiting with their cars, having come through the lines over a marked road. On the other side were the Allied cars and the sleigh of a car now belonging to Prince Bernard. It is the car which belonged to Seyss-Inquart and has been captured.

Jan Visits his Parents

Jan has to delay his trip west for two more days. On May 8, he finally reaches Rotterdam and the home of his parents and two youngest brothers, Martien and Nico.

May 8. The car is immediately surrounded by a huge crowd. I knocked at the door and knocked again. In the meantime the crowd had taken me, shoulder high, shouting a *Nederlander*. They sang *Oranje Boven, Long Live Holland*, etc. Nico and Martien came out. They looked thin and worn but delighted to see me. Members of the resistance stood arm-in-arm to protect my car while my cases were taken out. The driver added two loaves of bread, which caused the crowd to give huge "ohs," like the Eindhoven people seeing their first fireworks.

My father had come down the high and steep stairs, a frail old figure, wearing a collar twice the size of his neck. He was too moved to say anything. I went up and on the third floor of these flats, a very old, thin little woman stood waiting, tears already flowing. I could not say anything and just kissed the ash grey cheeks, just a skin over bones. I let her cry, till Martien, good lad, took her to a seat.

"Dinner" was just ready. "We have potatoes and Len has brought us a whole lot of white beans." Gravy without fat was supposed to help wash it down. Two tins of bully beef soon changed the menu.* My God, *kindje*, it has been terrible to see your own people hungry. Hungry, *schatje*, more than that. My good mother cannot even swallow the bread from

---

* Bully beef is canned corned beef, a standard military ration during World War II. Source: http://www.thefreedictionary.com/bully+beef.

Sweden. It's too dry. There has been no fat, or butter, or margarine for weeks.

Let me spare you too many details. It has been too much for me. *Lieve kindje*, there is hunger here so terrible, so frightful, that I should like to run away, as a coward, because I cannot bear the sight any longer. There is no bread in The Hague, and people are starving. Of course, there are those who have something, but the very large majority is starving. Things are worse than I had expected. Most of the food dropped has so far has failed to reach the people in Rotterdam and The Hague. There is no transport for distribution.*

Let me go back to my family. Sjef and Jac are still in Germany. Ben, Len's husband, has not been heard of since November, when he was deported to Nürnberg [Nurenburg, Germany]. Len, of course, broke down when she saw me. Martien and Nico have had miraculous escapes. Nico twice saved his skin by lying six hours in a milk van while the Gestapo searched the houses around. Several times the Gestapo steps have sounded on our stairs. My father has had the revolver on his chest when he was

---

* In Rotterdam, the first food parcels are dropped on April 28 on the outskirts of the town, in Terbregge. Problems with transport mean that many do not receive food packages until several weeks later, after the liberation. Source: J.L. van der Pauw. *Rotterdam in de Tweede Wereldoorlog* (Amsterdam: Boom, 2006).

asked to give away Elly's [German-born] husband's
hiding place.*

The family has gone through hell, and then they
tell me that they have been comparatively fortunate!
Others have suffered so much more. Several of the
uncles have died, one might say of hunger. It nor-
mally starts with some illness, to which the body
can find no resistance. One tremendous blessing is
that the babies look so well. Everything has gone to
them. That at least applies to our family.

I know this report is incoherent. But I just see before
me again those hordes of urchins, amongst whom
some lovely little faces, asking me for some bread.
And I cannot give it. My heart bleeds, *kindje. Ik ben
er kapot van.* Some food has been promised for next
Friday. I am dreading the days to come.

Kindjelief, ask people to send what they can spare.
There is such need in this land. No punishment can
ever wipe out the crime the Germans have commit-
ted against my country and its people.

May 11. Let me say that the dreadful experiences
of Rotterdam have in many ways put a brake on

---

* Theo van den Meiracker, the husband of Jan's youngest sister Wies, managed to
avoid the *razzias.* Family lore has it that on at least one occasion, he ventured outside,
disguised as a woman, to take his baby daughter Ria for a walk. An aunt would follow
at a distance in case he was caught by the Germans. Ria is one of the many children
whose baby food included tulip bulbs. Source: Ria van den Meiracker. Verbal communication. Spring 2008.

my happiness of this unforgettable return home to the towns and villages I know so well. These past few days have been the most momentous I have ever experienced. Final impressions cannot yet be formulated. It has all been too much. The picture of my mother rather haunts me. She has not deserved such sufferings. We must do something about it.

After a tiring morning conference, the American driver and I set out for the capital, Amsterdam. The town was as always a beehive of people. This afternoon the first food was distributed. Thousands of children sang patriotic songs on the Dam, where 10 days before Gerbrandy had a bigger reception than de Gaulle in Paris on the day of its liberation. This is the heart of Holland.

We drove back via Haarlem where I saw Sjf and Til.* Were they pleased. The two eldest children were on a farm in Friesland. Til had worried of course when they were cut off. All looked well. Sjef had managed until quite recently. He even had some English cigarettes! And that is saying something. For if there is one thing people are begging for it's for a smoke. They pay any price for an English cigarette. The Dutch have become beggars. I say it with a certain amount of shame. Our car cannot halt anywhere without men or women coming up and begging for

---

* Sjef and Til Scholte, cousins on Jan's mother's side of the family.

just one cigarette. I have given away hundreds and hundreds.*

Tomorrow, I hope to get back in my billet, and to a spot of rest. Also to a warm meal which I have not had since Monday night! Sandwiches and sandwiches, bully beef and bully beef. The greatest treat for the hungry, the worry of the spoilt like myself.

Jan and Marie's Peace-Time Baby

Jan's excitement at the momentous events unfolding around him is somewhat overshadowed by his concerns for Marie and the new baby, who is due any day—who for all he knows may have already arrived.

> **May 13.** This afternoon I go to Brussels by car, then by train to Paris for a meeting tomorrow. I cannot say how terribly disappointed I am that there was no letter waiting for me in Eindhoven. I take it that our baby has not yet arrived. I have never been so anxious to have news and never been so neglected by the mail. You, poor thing, have no doubt also been very much without letters just at a time when you like to have news.

The purpose of the trip to Paris is to attend a conference of national chief press censors—the first SHAEF meeting that Jan

---

* Not only does Jan get cigarettes as part of his NAAFI rations, most of the "care" packages he receives from Marie also include cigarettes.

attends not as a captain but as a major (he was promoted on May 6).

> **May 14.** All day we conferred. I spoke on behalf of the Dutch and took decisions, which I'll have to pass on to my government. In the evening we were the guests of the SHAEF at a private dinner party in the Hotel Chatham. I shall not tantalize you with a description. Believe me, it was excellent. Being the first to give a toast, I had a clear field. It was all very agreeable and pally and we went on till midnight.

SHAEF meeting of the national press censors. Paris. May 14, 1945.
Jan is second from left.

Marie Bernadette is born on May 15. That same day, Jan, still in Paris, writes Marie:

> **May 15.** The baby must surely have arrived by now. I cannot get over the fact that I have no communication with you. Whatever may be the position, accept my love and kisses, either as good luck ones or kisses of congratulations and gratitude. I am writing this on the terrace of *Café de la Paix,* at the corner of Place de l'Opéra and the Boulevard, drinking a grape juice, while the sun is pouring transpiration on my face. It is good to be here. It is still Paris. There may be no taxis, and the roads may be comparatively quiet, there may be too many Americans and Allied military; it is still Paris and French.
>
> I phoned Thérèse [Marie's older half-sister] and arranged to meet her (if possible with Maurice and children) in *Café de la Paix.* Sat at the café from three to five o'clock with Maurice, Thérèse, Marie-Thérèse and Jean-Louis. They have had a tiring time and are still experiencing difficult days due to the great food shortage. Jean-Louis has become a fine boy who speaks very little English though understands nearly all. Marie-Thérèse is charming—she has got the sweetest voice possible. I felt very sorry I had nothing to give the children. For them my visit must have been an anti-climax.

On May 18, Jan learns about his daughter's birth from the Huysmans, but he still has no word from Marie.

> **May 20.** Whitsun [Pentecost]. The weird thing is that the only news I have is Huysmans' announcement. For all I know I may have a son, or twins. All day long my thoughts wonder away to your nursing home and the children. I have to restrain myself from asking again all the questions about you and the baby which will remain in my mind till your letters have told me all about yourself and the new baby. Somehow I feel that everything is well but I want to see it in your handwriting before I feel happy.

> **May 21.** Whit Monday. Still no news from you! Can you imagine that I feel unhappy? I don't mind all the uncertainty about my work. I don't even mind working full time and more during the Whitsun holiday, but I hate being without any news from you. *Lieve schatje,* this uncertainty whether everything is all right makes it impossible for me to concentrate.

Finally, he receives the long-awaited letter from Marie.

> **May 24.** *Lief vrouwtje* of mine, you really are the sweetest most marvellous little woman in the world. I almost cried out of happiness when I read about the birth of our Mia. Only now nine days after the event the news has become real. How did you manage to write on the day of her birth? You are an amazing kid. The lightest baby of all! How is that

possible? A little Treesje, and even more doll-like! My congratulations, *liefje*, and many thanks. It is hard to write all these things. I ought to be with you. See you looking fit and well in your private room! See that little doll of yours, see it surrounded by three curious little visitors, ever asking.

May 25. *Lief meiske,* I feel happy mainly because all my worries about you and our Mia are over. Your cheerful letters have bucked me up no end. If only I could come out have a look at you! I only now realize that I was in Paris when our baby was born. Tell the little ones that I congratulate them with their fine little sister, and that I expect them to look after her. I wish Treesje could write to me her own description of her impressions. Is it not a shame that I have to miss their reaction? Duty can be hard and almost unfair.

In early June, the baby's godfather, Ton Speekenbrink, brings news of Marie and the baby.

June 2. Are you at home or still in the nursing home? Even that I don't know. Ton has confirmed that you were looking really well and that our Mia is indeed a delightful doll with masses of black hair. "She is like her mother, thank your lucky stars," Ton said. Well she could do worse.

June 7. A letter today! A very happy cheery one, written the day of the baptism of our Mia. I can so well imagine you feeling delighted with your little treasure all dressed up in her beautiful gown. I hope her hair remains dark and that she may be the image of you in every respect.

Although the baby is christened Marie Bernadette, she will at first be known as Mia, briefly Marie, and within the year as Bernadette.

On June18, Jan finally meets his five-week-old daughter—just in time for her first smile.

> **June 18 [Marie's diary].** Jan unexpectedly home—phoned 4 p.m. from Waterloo [station].

> **June 22 [Marie's diary].** Baby's first smile.

> **June 25 [Marie's diary].** Jan back to The Hague.

As soon as Jan is back in his hotel in The Hague, he writes Marie.

> **June 26.** I am sitting once again on my bed, with my little table drawn near, ready for a late evening talk with you as of old. At 10:30 I finished work. Pretty good going for a first day's effort. Now I want to tell you all about it as I was able to last week: tell of my experiences, express my fears and hopes and think aloud.
>
> You should definitely get ready to move to Holland this year. It sounds selfish, but I feel that I need you here, when I have to be here. Do you want me to look back upon last week? Being with you. I talked brazenly

about you and the little ones staying in our little village. Hardly gone a day and I am already weakening.

Lieve kindje, thank you for last week. I know you have been busier through my presence, and by Jove, I could not imagine all that you have to do all day long, but I have so happily felt "at home." I feel better for it. And you?

Tell the little ones that I count on them helping you lots, when I am away. Tell them that I count on them putting their toys away every night after tea. Give them my blessing.

Marie with Bernadette. England. Spring, 1946.

For the remainder of the year, Jan manages short visits to Wraysbury every four weeks or so. For now, despite numerous discussions, the question of when Marie and the children should join Jan in Holland remains unsolved. A letter written after one such visit expresses clearly his awe at how well Marie manages the house and their four children. In July he writes:

> **July 30.** Give me all the worries in the world rather than the need of looking after the domestic side of a family.

Jan's Ongoing Role in the *Militair Gezag*

The war is over but Jan is still in military service. Within two weeks after liberation, he is posted to The Hague.

> **May 18.** I was called to General Kruls and ordered to take Huizinga's place as acting head of the Information Section of the *Militair Gezag*. Huizinga has been dismissed. All my objections were ignored and I was simply ordered to take charge. It will mean a heck of a lot of unpleasant and thankless work. It also means a final liquidation of my Eindhoven home. I may do that this weekend. What a fag! This new assignment had quite spoiled my chances to come and see you for the time being.

As head of Section XI of the post-war *Militair Gezag* (effective May 25), Jan—because of his promotion—is now responsible for press and publicity, the import of books, *Radio Herrijzend Nederland,* and ANEFO photo service.[83] In essence, the task consists of the gradual transfer of these services from the military to the civilian sector—as Jan indicates, an administrative nightmare.

A pleasant surprise is the location of Jan's new office in the Binnenhof, the 15th-century parliament buildings of Holland.

> **May 31.** I am writing this from my room at the *Binnenhof.* Here it is peaceful as in the Inner Temple in London. Never before have I realized the serene beauty of our parliament buildings as I do now, when quite unexpectedly my work has to be done from a room overlooking the old square, facing the Hall of Knights (Ridderzaal), represented in our photo album, I believe, with you standing on its steps.
>
> Everybody is already grumbling and nobody is satisfied. The hangover after the liberation is beginning. My task is to reduce possible tensions to a minimum. I might well break my neck if not my health. (Don't worry; I can stand a hell of a lot!) This morning I had my first bread. Living on iron ration biscuits is no joke. Food is finding its way to the people very slowly indeed. But there is at least something.

Jan is housed in a hotel with fellow SHAEF censors and gets his meals at a military mess.

> **May 25.** I changed my hotel today. Although I had a room reserved for me in Centraal, I moved, at my own wish, to a lousy little third-rate hotel, where my SHAEF censors are established. In this new room,

there is hardly any light and only one very wonky cupboard. I am glad I can lock two of my cases.

May 29. The talk today has been fleas and since dinner I have been feeling itches all over. Fleas are general all over Holland. My boast that they have better material to work on seems to have been more than false. One or two fleas seem to have settled somewhere. Since Eindhoven I have not had a bath. One poor effort to have a stand up wash-all-over was partly frustrated by the realization a little late that my curtains hardly hid my activities. Something is going to be laid on to enable us to have a bath. I'll go in any queue for that.

My friends are drinking downstairs. I supplied my NAAFI bottle of gin, but feel too tired to stay on, especially as I wanted a word with you before going to bed. Talking about bed, I have sheets in this hotel, but in the Centraal Hotel, where the *Militair Gezag* is and where I should be, no sheets are provided. Most officers seem to carry sheets. If only I had been wise when I had a chance to buy them in Brussels.

Ongoing Civilian Hardship

Jan's letters cover not only his adjustment to his new work assignments. but also a first-hand account of the aftermath of the *Honger Winter* and the ongoing hardships facing the civilian population.

May 18. This afternoon, I stole two hours to race to Rotterdam. I found my good mother ill and weak. I brought eggs and flowers from friends. They couldn't understand that I couldn't stay. My brother Jac has been in every day hoping to catch me. At [a friend's home] I dropped off two cases of food from his brother in Brabant. I had to move the cases to the living room as he was too weak to lift them. His sister, about 50, was in bed with hunger edema, and unable to take any of the food. She begged me not to tell her brother in Brabant. More and more cases of this disastrous disease are coming to light.*

May 25. Returning from Eindhoven, I stopped at home for a moment to deliver Mrs. Huysmans' parcel of food (butter, honey, etc.) and also Miss Lundie's parcel. Tell Miss Lundie that everything came in useful, especially the little shoes, for nephews and nieces.** Mother was still looking very seedy. Martien is coming round and looks fine.

Len had just called in that her husband Ben had reached Breda safely. Just in time, since she was getting really in a bad way and could hardly eat any

---

* By the end of the war, an estimated 100,000–150,000 Dutch are suffering from hunger edema. The death from famine for the country as a whole is estimated at 16,000–22,000. Keith Lowe, *Savage Continent: Europe in the Aftermath of World War II*. (New York: MacMillan, 2012) 36.

** In response to Jan's request for care packages from England, Wraysbury friends have been collecting clothing for the Dutch. Miss Lundie, the principal of Treesje's school, is particularly generous in collecting and forwarding donations.

more. Sjef, too, has reached Limburg in a convoy from Germany. You can well imagine the rejoicing at home.

As Jac and Martha had missed me on the two previous occasions, I went to see them for a moment. Were they delighted! Thea, the sweetest little girl you could imagine, was really wild with joy. Paul too is a really fine fellow, slightly pale but looking fit. Jac has become an old man, hardly recognizable. He has really had a tough time. His months in Germany have put years on him. And then the constant worry about Gestapo visits. He had false identity papers in his house, which was a constant source of intense concern. As always, their house looked neat and tidy. The top floor, however, has partly been wrecked as they had to remove timber to use as fuel for fire.*

Years later, Thea, age 11 at the time, remembers this visit, recalling that her *Oom Jan* brought several tins of food. They were so hungry that they ate the cold beans right out of the can.[84] Paul, then only eight years old, would like to forget the long winter alone with his mother and sister with barely enough food to survive, no fuel, and no medication. Anything of value was bartered for food: for instance, his father's stamp collection in exchange for a sack of

---

* Not only does Rotterdam not have coal, but from late November 1944 to late April 1945 only soup kitchens have gas for cooking. These kitchens close down in late April 1945 when they no longer have the food needed to prepare the thin watery soup so many relied on for minimal daily sustenance. Source: J.L. van der Pauw. *Rotterdam in de Tweede Wereldoorlog* (Amsterdam: Boom, 2006).

potatoes. Like others, he sifted through crumbled street asphalt to find pieces of coal.[85]

June 3. Pleasant Sunday afternoon trip to Rotterdam. My laundry was waiting for me. Un-ironed of course, as there is no heating. How they wash, I don't know, as they have no washing brush. Could we get one? Found mother looking slightly better. Nico and Martien in shorts sunbathing on the roof with Nico's girl in bathing suit (forget my frowns—I am too old-fashioned). Wies and Theo visiting, plus charming baby daughter. Sjef not yet returned, but news received from Roosendaal through an uncle of mine. He and his young wife and son are sure to be in difficult straits. What is one to do!

I have just finished my second meal at home. Absolutely staggering to see Martien and Nico go through their potatoes, and the tinned meat. Everybody begins to look better. The new food has created a fresh appetite. The rations plus my additions are at present ample to prepare good meals. Also, the grocer, greengrocer, and milkman know that they get one cigarette a day! Only the heating arrangements spoil everything. No electricity, so far, no coal, and no wood. Martien has been able to buy an old door, which now serves as fuel so that they can cook the food.

I shall be staying the night here, which pleases my mother no end. It is strange sitting at home, somehow more a welcome visitor than one of the family.

Jac is the one who looks poorest. Absolutely worn out. He is walking in the most terrible pair of shoes which cannot possibly be repaired. I wonder whether I have a decent pair of non-army shoes which you could send me for him. As you know I have a good array of shoes and boots, which will last quite a time after my demobilization. There is also a great demand for toothpaste on the part of Martien and Nico. Could you send me some?

When Sjef finally makes it back to Rotterdam, Jan is shocked at the appearance of his once handsome 30-year-old brother: "My God, those two years, mainly spent in digging, have wrecked this boy."

June 6. The Dutch in general begin to realize only now in what sort of chaos the Germans have landed them. You cannot picture such chaos. No trains, no buses, no trams, hardly any telephone, few wireless sets, newspapers of a single small sheet only, food just sufficient to manage, but no coal, gas, or electricity to cook (our military hotel has some electricity), no earthly chance to buy foot-wear or clothing, or for that matter anything at all. Very few shops are open. Offices work a few hours as there is no economic life yet. A frightful state of things. Dissatisfaction must grow. I only hope people don't lose their common sense. A few may, and may cause trouble.

A Job Offer in the Dutch Foreign Office

Jan's earlier worries about not being employable after the war prove to have been unnecessary. In June, Van Kleffens, now the Minister of Foreign Affairs in The Hague, offers Jan a position as chief of the Foreign Office's press service. Despite some initial hesitation, Jan accepts.

> **June 27.** This morning, I had a moment to talk with minister Beel [then the Minister of Interior, later the Prime Minister], who strongly advised me to accept Van Kleffens' post. Well, I did. This morning I met with the two ministers of the Foreign Office, Van Kleffens and Van Royen, and I decided that I was prepared to become their press chief (Chief of the Foreign Office's Press Service). A hell of a lot of detail remains to be settled. It is all rather vague, in fact. Would it be wise? Can I set up an efficient organization, when the market is so small as far as available "bodies" are concerned? I know you will bless my difficult decisions and adjust as well as you can.
>
> I shall have a hell of a lot of spadework to do before things are settled. All the arrangements for the foreign press are in my hand, and nothing has been done as yet. I feel quite nervy about things. You'd better keep on saying a few little prayers.

No sooner has Jan agreed to the press chief position at the Foreign Office than a number of other job offers pour in.

June 27 (continued). Last night, [Henry] Kuypers [one of the directors of the *Maasbode*] called at my hotel to persuade me to join his staff, promising me trips and what not.

Bernard Meyerink, the former financial editor of the *Maasbode*, has invited me to become financial correspondent in London for a big purely financial paper which has started in Amsterdam. He guarantees good pay too. And I had just accepted Van Kleffens' invitation. What a life. *Quel embarras de choix!* Who would have thought that? Should I go back on my acceptance of Van Kleffens' offer? London does attract me so much.

July 9. Just tonight a cable reached me to accept the post of director of the Dutch news service, ANEP, in Australia at acceptable, really favorable terms. The end of it all may be that I land in between two chairs, if not in between four chairs. What am I to do about it all? All these posts require expert knowledge, which I shall have to master. What I really want is a job which I can fulfil, without ever worrying whether I can cope with it. And that job is not to be found. There does not seem to be any reason to fear that I cannot feed my family for the time being. In these stages, a word with Pelt might help. Good night, darling. Tomorrow may be a decision day for our future. May your prayers guide me.

July 10. This morning I had a two-hour conversation with Van Kleffens and Van Royen. Van Kleffens guarantees that I get my opportunity to do some travelling to foreign ports, but my domicile will remain at The Hague. Taxation will be terribly high. *Kindje*, we better wait and see, and not worry too much. I'll have to learn French; you'll have to learn Dutch. You'll have to have a maid and/or someone for the children. It will be a completely new life with all its thrills and complications. Honestly, I don't know whether I have done wise. I am going to earn less, though for Holland it is a considerable salary, and we'll be forced to do a lot of entertaining, both at home and in town. You are in for a busy time.

Marie may have to learn Dutch, but Jan is concerned that his schoolboy French won't suffice now that he works for the Foreign Office.

August 1. I returned to the office today to find a pile of difficulties, which took me all day to untangle. In the midst of it, a French journalist landed on me who spoke French only. There were people in my room who spoke French like their mother language, and heard me mumble away in my pidgin French. Most embarrassing. Tomorrow I am lunching with him in the officers' club. On my own, I may do better.

September 9. Talking about learning French, I went to the *Vieux Doelen* last night to look up Ton Speekenbrink. He was dining with a friend. I joined them for coffee and a *pousse*. He has his worries too! One of them is, and don't think he overdoes it, his knowledge or rather lack of knowledge of French. At international meetings the language is, more often than not, French. Ton has made up his mind that he is going to take French conversation classes. So shall I. We may do it together.

The Allied "Occupation"

The many young American, Canadian, and other Allied troops have brought freedom, food, and the inevitable fraternization with civilians. Jan expresses his concern about what he sees in Dutch as well as Belgian cities.

> **Brussels, August 21.** Plenty of prostitutes about and plenty of young kids hanging around the soldiers. Two large prophylactic stations on the main boulevard tell a story by the fact of their existence. God help any country's young women where there are thousands of troops on leave about.

> **The Hague, August 26.** I had a first-class tea in the officers' club in The Hague, where nearly every table was occupied by Allied officers with good-looking girls. It was an eyeful right and left. I was fortunate enough to be able to join a table of one Dutch officer with a smart girl. I gathered that he

has been living with her these past few weeks. Well, he could have made a worse choice. I doubt whether his wife agrees. I could but think of the marvellous thundering sermon I heard this morning, based on today's gospel, in which the young Dutch women and the unscrupulous military were taken to task. The priest did not mince words. I have never heard such blunt words in church on sex and excesses. It is a fact that the sights in The Hague's squares and parks and fields are revolting. The prayer is going up in Holland: From the new occupation, deliver us, O Lord.

Wraysbury or The Hague?

Now that Jan has accepted a position in The Hague, the big question facing him and Marie is how soon Marie and the children should join him in Holland. The main obstacle is that the coming winter in Holland might be very hard on the children. Treesje is only six, Colette is four, Jantje barely three, and Marie Bernadette still an infant. There's a very good chance that this will be a winter without any coal or other fuel, power outages, and perhaps major food shortages. Jan, like Marie, is hesitant to subject the children to these hardships if it isn't absolutely necessary.

As acute as the housing shortage in The Hague is now, it may get worse. In March, the British Royal Air Force mistakenly destroyed the residential section of Bezuidenhout. More than 500 residents were killed, and more than 3,200 homes destroyed. (The intent had been to destroy the V-launching equipment and sites near The Hague.)[86] A nearby neighborhood, Benoordenhout—as well as the area adjacent to the Scheveningen sea resort—was completely taken over by the Germans and heavily fortified. The residents were evacuated, and quite a few of the larger homes were taken over by German officers.[87] It is in this area as well that Seyss-Inquart made his home, in the Clingendael estate. By summer 1945, many former residents have not returned and some homes are still available, although many have suffered significant damage.

The question of when the family should come to Holland is one that Jan and Marie ask themselves over and over again. During Jan's brief June visit, they decide that Marie should stay in England until the situation improves in Holland. Jan, however, is barely back in Holland when he changes his mind.

> **June 25.** It looks as if you should definitely get ready to move to Holland this year, as I cannot maintain my family in England [on my current salary]. It sounds selfish, but I feel that I need you here, when I have to be here. Do you want me to look back upon last week? Being with you, I talked brazenly about you and the little ones staying in our little village.

> **September 1.** If only you could come over now for a week or so, while I still have a car. You could even stay in our hotel though I have not seen any mothers with three-month old babies. Once I lose the car, it will be very hard to move about. You'd better learn driving quickly. I need a driver!

September 7. The most important thing, however, is that there may be a house available for me in the near future. I am going to see it tomorrow. What am I to do if it is a good one? I am inclined to take it, which would mean your coming over this year as I cannot keep it empty for half a year. I know that you will be much better off in Wraysbury this winter, but the prospects of getting a house are diminishing every week. I wish you were here to help me make up my mind. Is there no earthly prospect of your coming over with the baby? You might discuss it with Mrs. Pelt. She would give you soundest advice.

September 20. It seems incredible that it's only a few weeks ago since I left you and the little ones. Everything seems so distant again. More than ever, especially more than when I was in Brabant, do I feel that distance between myself and my home. I cannot get resigned to the fact that this will have to remain the position till next summer or at least spring. Somehow I am rather funking the thought of it. I feel so much more a stranger here than I did in the south. The Hague is so big in comparison. In Eindhoven I had my "home" so near to the mess and office and other friends where I could call in any odd hour. Loneliness is being felt much more in a big city than in a small country town.

Miss Schalij [Jan's secretary] has offered to give the utmost help to you, when you have to set up house here. She realizes that I shall be completely hopeless arranging the possibilities to cook, or to light the place, and she simply ordered me to ask you to let her know in time the things that will have to be arranged. That is all very well, but one must have a house first, and then we can start dealing with cooking facilities, etc.

In the end, Jan and Marie decide that for the sake of the children, it is best if Marie remains in England until the following spring.

November 4. You ought to put in one great effort to come over here for say one week, ten days, just to have a look around. Can it be done? You bring the baby along. I don't know where you can stay, but I'll fix that. Do tell me whether it is at all possible. Is there any one person able and willing to run our place with three young children? If yes, is it possible for you to fly with Marietje and stay here, e.g., with the Baerts, with the Huysmans, in my Rotterdam home even if you like* . That side of the picture we'll fix.

I am convinced it would mean a marvellous break for you and for me. At the moment I can still command transport. After December it would be impossible. Do think it over very seriously. Despite

---

* Jan and Marie's Wraysbury friends, Remi and Toos Baert now live in The Hague where Remi is attached to the Belgian Embassy. The Huysmans too have moved to the Hague as, in 1945, Huysmans is appointed the Dutch Minister of Finance.

all the strain of arranging things, I am convinced that such a change would do you no end of good. You would meet a very interesting crowd and I shall be happy to take as much time off as possible to gad about a bit.

On December 5, Marie takes a flight from London to the Valkenburgh airport, north of The Hague, for a 10-day visit. Marie's days in Holland are filled with family visits, dinner and dances with friends, and the ongoing but still fruitless house search. A week later, Jan travels to England to spend Christmas and New Year's with Marie and the children.

The year ends with the hope that in 1946 Marie and the children will join Jan in The Hague.

CHAPTER IX

REUNITED IN HOLLAND
May 1946 to March 1947

By January 1946, the quasi-military apparatus of the *Militair Gezag* is gradually winding down. It will cease to exist in March. Jan's role as press censor has ended. Although not yet officially demobilized, for all intents and purposes, he is once again a civilian.

Returning to The Hague after his Christmas break, Jan's first order of business is to find civilian housing for himself. He also continues to search for a home for the family. He focuses the family house hunting primarily on the Benoordenhout area of The Hague, and to a lesser extent in nearby Scheveningen and Wassenaar—the latter are somewhat less desirable because of their distance from the Dutch Foreign Office. Once Marie and the children have joined him in The Hague, Jan expects to be commuting to and from work by bike, and coming home midday for lunch.

Life as a civilian

January 11, 1946. I was told that I really had no right to stay in military housing at Hotel Centraal. I am on "leave" without any military rights till the day of my demobbing. I don't know how to solve the problem, but one thing is certain, that I shall have to find accommodations almost immediately. Living in a hotel costs a packet of money, but it may be the best solution for electricity, food, and service. It is all very annoying, and this suddenness has rather overtaken me. I'll have a long talk with my colonel tomorrow.

January 13. Arrangements have been made for me to stay in Centraal for the next two weeks. Some peace of mind has returned to me as a consequence. Today I received my papers permitting me to wear civvies.

February 12. Yesterday, I moved into the [Hotel] Vieux Doelen. My room is really a little salon, with a bed in it and a washbasin, which can be closed off. There is only one cupboard, which cannot contain all my coats and shirts. The worst of the room is that it is situated on the first floor, which means that I have to keep the curtains closed when undressing and dressing. Furthermore, this corner room—the coldest in the house because of its three large windows at the sides of the square and side street—is drafty. I cannot say that I feel at home. For one thing the place is too expensive.

What has depressed me a great deal is that I cannot wear my civvies. I have no cufflinks for my shirt (I'll buy some here) and no socks. Every pair which is not mended and ready to give-away is moth-eaten. Everybody tells me that no doubt all my suits will gradually get affected as these things spread like hell. I have started brushing and what not but I am too clumsy to make a good job of it.

February 17. I still have to get used to being called *mijnheer* [Mr. or sir]. I see soldiers and am ready to return their salute. I miss the comfort of my battle dress. I have with great difficulty received my civilian ration cards for four weeks—without any meat coupons. Still, don't worry too much. You have your concerns. Just pray, pray to have our family reunited. I cannot tell you how much I miss you.

Yesterday afternoon I had a car waiting to take me to the owner of a house in the Waalsdorperweg. I flunked it. I simply did not dare to take the house, knowing it to be sombre and dark and not looking so well-to-do-ish as other houses of that price. Toos Baert's sister, who had also seen that house, refused to take it, as it was too dark!

March 3.I could have wept when the Waalsdorperweg house had gone. I could have had it. The same applies to the Ruychrocklaan house. I blame myself for not making up my mind. Prospects are now terribly

meager. I am completely at a loss as to what to do.
Every decent house, which is not a complete ruin, has
gone. It drives me crazy. I do my best not to think
about things too much. I so badly need my own
home, with you and the children. It sounds strange,
but I feel the distance much more now than during
my military days. I cannot imagine that it is only one
month since I saw you. Jantje is smiling at me from
that lovely photo in the deck chair. I realize that I am
abnormally fond of that little fellow. Last night I was
thinking that he'll get a good chance in life if I stick
to my job.

Jan Visits New York and Washington

In early March, Jan finally gets his wish to travel overseas. As Director
of the Information Service at the Foreign Office, he is required to
make periodic visits to Dutch Information Services abroad. The trip
starts with a 22-hour flight from Amsterdam to New York.

> **March 8.** We are halfway between Eire and
> Newfoundland. I was asleep when coffee was served
> by a magazine-cover stewardess, pearly teeth, blonde
> curls, round curves and all that. Pity. I was fast asleep.
> Not that I didn't fancy looking at this treat, but I
> could do with sleep. The lights are out, and only my
> own bulb is throwing light like the steady light of a
> cinema usherette when looking for a lost glove. The
> plane is just like a small cinema. Comfortable *fau-
> teuils*, 2 and 2, 12 couples each side. It is warm. Our

beauty just lowered the temperature a bit. Most of us have a woollen cover over our legs. Stretchable slippers were provided with piles of *Life, Time, Colliers,* etc. We had sandwiches and martinis over the Irish Channel.

Shannon was the Irish point of touching down. Just an hour to have a couple of drinks, dinner, and a postcard to write home. We invested our first dollars in cigars. Shannon, just an airport, but typical Irish scenes did not fail. Charming Irish brogue waitresses and canteen girls. Two Franciscan priests, sandaled, dining with a family and enjoying life.

Everything on this trip has been first class. I have to go over my sad departure. Around me: wives, sweethearts, friends, kissing the travellers, as I have never seen in any international railway station. It made me realize all of a sudden that this was rather a big trip, and that I, once again, was alone. I felt a pang of sadness when I walked out of the enclosure to the plane, alone, hugging my attaché case.

Still about five hours to go. The plane is snoring its way forward. We have been shown how to put our life belts on, where the four exits are, and how we should try to get into our four dinghies. What hope! I don't want that experience. There are so many good things left in this difficult life. Like going back again to your loved ones, sharing pleasures and worries with your *vrouwtje.*

Jan's first letter from New York City presents his initial impressions.

March 9. The skyscrapers are high indeed. The roads are full of life and ever moving. The shops are full. Plenty of cigarettes and candy. Fantastic prices. The rooms are terribly warm. Everybody is sipping iced water. For sheer nerves I am smoking my throat to bits. Yellow taxis are making a constant din. I must see something of New York before I leave. Leave! I have hardly arrived!

March 10. I dined last night at an American banker's home. What a home. It reminds me of the pictures. American pictures don't seem to overdo the richness of wealthy American homes. I had that invitation through Hans Hermans of the *Maasbode*.[88] The charming family was Catholic too.

We had plenty to drink, eat, and talk about. At 11, Hermans and I took a cab to Broadway. An unbelievable sight. I have never thought it possible that so many colored lights could be squeezed into or over one street. We walked about with the many thousands, who on Saturday night make Broadway the most crowded street in the world. At midnight we almost decided go to a show, but I felt so tired that we did not after all.

I slept till 9, had breakfast of grapefruit, bacon and egg, toast and marmalade, and milk. The restaurant in this club is on the 20th floor! One can order out of a great variety of things. If you see the glut of food over here, one wonders why so many people are starving in other countries. All day long, people are eating and chewing gum and drinking fruit juice. This is a world of its own. I am concentrating on oranges and milk! I am off to Washington tomorrow.

March 12. Yesterday evening I spent at Daniel Schor's house, talking and taking in impressions.[89] We were, of course, entertained most lavishly. One is either rich or poor in this weird country. This morning I left from Pennsylvania Railroad Station for Washington. A few hours' journey. I was booked a seat in a lounge car with bar! I had an excellent dinner: tomato juice, chicken, cheese, and coffee in the dining car. Washington made a first-class impression on me—no skyscrapers. Just houses with gardens. This town has more than 50 percent Negroes.

The Embassy has reserved a hotel for me. I'm settled for at least five days in a small but comfortable room, plus as always a bathroom. I had intended to leave again tomorrow night, but there are so many people to see that I have already postponed my departure until Wednesday morning. The American ambassador in The Hague had cabled my arrival to the State Department with instructions that a few people should see me!

Washington is a town like the best part of Paris. I should not mind living here. Maybe I'll find time to see something of the town this afternoon. I quite enjoy the travelling part of my journey. The business side is giving me great concern, and that is sure to become worse as time progresses. There are not many general impressions which would interest you. I'll try to sum up a few. Everybody has beautiful, white teeth. One talks about the shortage of motorcars as we do of bicycles. The strike has stalled production to the extent of creating a shortage. Drinks are plentiful. I am now on "old-fashioneds." The American girls when attractive are very attractive. The plentiful food soon becomes boring as a result of the careless mass-produced way of preparing.

Jan's letters do not indicate the exact date of his return to The Hague but imply a return no later than April.

Marie and Treesje Visit Holland

In early May 1946, Marie makes her second visit to Holland to search for a house and to celebrate Jan's parents' 40th wedding anniversary. This time she brings Treesje with her. They stay with Jan in the Vieux Doelen hotel, where, on May 5, their room gives them a ringside seat of The Hague celebrating the first anniversary of the country's liberation.

In preparation for the coming move to Holland, Marie and Jan arrange for Treesje to spend a month in Rotterdam with her non-English-speaking grandparents.

Nico and with Treesje and with Thea and Paul (Jac and Martha's children).
Rotterdam. May 3, 1946.

A few days after Marie's return to England, Jan attends a reception honoring Churchill at the Royal Palace in Amsterdam.[90] Guests include some 60 journalists, mostly Dutch. A highlight of Churchill's visit is his welcome in Rotterdam. Thousands upon thousands line the streets to get a glimpse of his motorcade.

Treesje and her cousin, Thea, well remember this event. Perched high on Nico and Jac's shoulders, they see not only Churchill but also Jan, in one of the jeeps following Churchill's car.

De ontvangst van de Nederlandsche journalisten ten Paleize

Reception for Churchill and Dutch journalists at the Royal Palace in Amsterdam. Jan is second from left (with his arms crossed). May 10, 1946.*

In early June, Jan takes Treesje back to England for what will be his last visit to Wraysbury. Back in The Hague, he writes:

---

* The photo appears in a small publication describing Churchill's short visit to the Netherlands in May, 1946: A.B.M. Brans en E. Cancrinus,: *Winston Churchill bezoekt Nederland. 8 mei tot en met 13 mei 1946* (Leiden: A.W. Sijthoff's Uitgeversmaatschappij, 1946).

The photographer is unknown and the former Sijthoff publishing company has since been taken over by Luiting-Sijfhoff Publishers in Amsterdam, They, however, no longer have the copyright to this particular photo. So long as the photographer is unknown, The Netherlands' Pictoright Institute sees no objection to the use of this photo. Source: E-mail dated July 19, 2014 from Marcel van de De Graaf, the Pictoright Institute. m.vandegraaf@pictoright.nl

June (no specific date). It is a strange and almost sad feeling that my departure leaves no thought of regret in the minds of any of the children. They just take it for granted, that I come and go. Maybe better that way, though I feel that I am not sufficiently well in with them.

The Move to Holland

At long last, Jan finds a house on the Josef Israelslaan in The Hague. The children don't know that from 1943 to 1945, the street had a different name. Refusing to honor a Jewish painter—Josef Israëls (1756–1807)—the Germans renamed the street. During the war, the street is known as the Thorn Prikkerlaan—after the Dutch art nouveau artist, Thorn Prikker (1868–1932).[91]

Marie loves Jan's description of the location of the house: a short bike ride to Jan's office, within easy walking distance of the Sint Paschalis church and school, and close to both the Baerts and the Huysmans. The size and location of the house—on a tree-lined street leading to a park—make up for its lack of a front garden and its miniscule north-facing back garden.

Less than a month before the planned move, Marie receives a distressing note from Jan. He has had discouraging news from the owner of the property: Toos Baert's father, a Dutch industrialist.

> **June 28.** Sit down and hold tight. Our house won't be ready till September! I phoned tonight. Mrs. Boes answered. "Well," I said, cheerfully, "the family hope to get in at the end of August." "My God," she said,

"how terrible, the house won't be ready until the end of September at the earliest. The plans for renovation have not yet been designed, what made you think it would only be six weeks?" I did not burst, I kept quiet, and asked to speak to Mr. Boes. In fact, I had given his name to the maid at first. Mrs. Boes was sent to the phone. Mr. Boes came on and I sort of raged a bit. Yes, he had said six weeks, but they had just started. It would be a little more, etc., etc. "But what about my furniture?" He offered to store it at his factory (he did not mention a price!), where Toos's furniture had been kept and looked after. That is at least one thing. *Schatje,* I feel terribly depressed about it all.

In mid-July, Marie and the children take the night boat to Holland. The plan is that they will stay with Jan's parents in their flat in Rotterdam while waiting for the house to be ready. Jan and Marie at first hesitate to accept his parents' invitation, but they are soon reassured by the warn welcome they receive.

> **July 2.** My people are thrilled with the invasion. I now realize to the full that they would have been terribly disappointed if their offer had not been accepted.

The flat with its three bedrooms—two of which are very small, can barely house four children and six adults (Jan's parents, Jan, Marie, Nico and Martien). Jan, Marie and the children share two bedrooms. Nico and Martien sleep on a daybed in the living room for the duration of the visit.

Marie and the children in Rotterdam. Summer1946.

As Jan is due for a holiday, he and Marie decide that this is a good time for him to visit Marie's relatives near Lyon, France. Jan hopes that being immersed in an all-French environment will help him brush up on his French. By early August, he is back again in Holland, slightly more comfortable about his French, somewhat rested, and well fed ("We had cream, real cream!"). Upon his return from France, he arranges to spend weekdays with an old friend in The Hague and to stay with the family on weekends,

When September rolls around, it is clear that the house won't be ready for another six to eight weeks. In a letter to Eileen Keegan, Marie describes her new life:

September 17 [Letter from Marie to Eileen Keegan]. They do not expect we'll be able to move for another six or eight weeks. This was an awful blow as we had been told mid-September. I have put the children in school here in Rotterdam. Treesje is in the second class with children of her own age and seems to be holding her own. She loves it, which is a great help. During August, I had a girl of 17 who came in for an hour every morning to give her a little lesson and I think that that helped her a good deal. Colette and Jantje go to a Montessori school. They are picking up their Dutch gradually. Colette says quite a few phrases and sentences. Jantje does so occasionally—as a great favor! Colette started her Dutch by swearing.

The food position now is generally speaking much better than in England! What is really terrible here is the clothing. There is not much in the shops and what there is of very poor quality and very expensive. Wool is just beginning to appear. Shoes are just hopeless. Many people have not yet had a shoe coupon. It is dreadful to see children walking about with no shoes—even in filthy weather or with the toes cut away because they're too small. Boys wear ladies' shoes, and of course many have clogs. Yesterday when it was pouring with rain, I saw many children with cotton dresses just covered with a short jacket—nothing on their heads! Treesje said that they placed a tub in the classroom and that all the children wrung their dresses out in it. When they'd finished the tub was full—isn't it frightful!

Jan stays at The Hague and comes here on weekends and an occasional evening. He gets a number of invitations in which I am often included. Now that I can leave the children, I have joined him occasionally. I've been to lunch at the Italian Embassy, and a cocktail at the Russian Embassy. Rather fun and a terrific experience! I've never seen so much food and drink collected together as there was there. As someone remarked—if that was what communism meant, he was all for it! At the Chinese Embassy, we ate with chopsticks.

The Move to The Hague

By mid-January 1947, the house is almost ready. Jan, meanwhile, is finding that Van Kleffens' promise that he would get to travel is not always a blessing. In late January, he returns to The Netherlands' Information Office in New York and visits their office in Ottawa. To his dismay, he learns that what was intended as a relatively short trip has been extended by another three weeks.

With the assistance of family and friends, especially the Husymans and the Baerts, Marie manages the move and all the associated red tape and inspections. Following one of her first visits to the new house, she describes her day to Jan.

January 24, 1947 [Letter from Marie to Jan]. It is midnight and I'm only just starting to write to you! I'm so busy! It is lovely. Went very proudly to our own house by bus. Found the house very clean. Telephone arrived. Men came to read meter for electric heater; measure fireplace for dining. Later the sweep called—chimneys have to be cleaned by law because of fire. Good night, *mijn lieve schatje*. You must be praying very hard for me because I feel so happy about everything.

A week later, Marie and the children move into their new home.

February 2 [Letter from Marie to Jan]. I do wish you were here. The first night in our new home. The children were all thrilled to bits. Bernadette was running all over, and they all went mad about their playroom. Good night, *schatjelief,* and thank you for our lovely house and everything that is in it—come and see it quickly.

In early March 1947, Jan returns from New York. The family's long separation is over.

It doesn't take long for the children to settle into their new home.
Photo taken on the occasion of Treesje's first communion. April 1947.

CHAPTER X

EPILOGUE

Jan, Marie, and the children spend four years in The Hague. A fifth child, Liduine, is born here in August 1948—the first child whom Jan gets to see on a regular basis throughout her early childhood.

The first few years in post-war Holland present many challenges. The children gradually adjust to a new language, to walks in a manicured park rather than rambles through the English countryside, and to a regimented and overcrowded school—crowding that lets up a little after the rebuilding of a number of bombed-out classrooms. Marie adjusts to running a household in a new country with ongoing food and clothing rationing, limited fuel, and sporadic household help. But these are minor drawbacks compared to her happiness at having Jan home again. As always, she fully supports Jan and does everything she can to make sure he doesn't have to worry about the domestic side of running a family. Jan, happy to be home with his beloved Marie at his side, adjusts to being a regular member of the family rather than an occasional visitor.

On Jan's behalf, Marie is excited about the travel he must do for the Foreign Office. She continues to write cheerful letters during his occasional long absences, including almost yearly trips to

Canada and New York. In late 1947, his travels include Central and South America—a trip that lasts almost three months, including a 10-day Atlantic crossing from New York to Rotterdam. After The Netherlands recognizes Indonesia's independence, Jan makes at least one trip to the former Dutch colony. In March 1950, he visits Djakarta, Makkasar (on the island of Sulawesi), and Bali. This time as well he returns by sea—a 20-day-journey. Marie writes, "We are all following your journey on the map. Little Liduintje continues to ask for Papa. At home and also when we are out, she'll suddenly say 'Papa? Papa? Papa out?' The older ones take it all for granted, but they don't forget to pray for you. We all say a little prayer before and after every meal."

Jan later tells his children that he could have accepted a post in Indonesia, but at that time he did not consider it a good place to raise young children. A post that Jan readily accepts, in 1951, is that of press and cultural counselor at The Netherlands Embassy in Brussels.

Brussels provides a wonderful change of pace for the family. By 1951, the post-war privations have lessened considerably, especially in Belgium, where the rebuilding of the country, because of lesser damage to the overall infrastructure, has been faster than in Holland.[92] Jan is pleased that this new position does not call for travel overseas. Most of the time, Marie has excellent household help and is able to join fully in the diplomatic whirl of dinners, cocktail parties, and related social events. But weekends are reserved for family activities. Any evening that they are at home, Jan and Marie play a quiet game of Scrabble or backgammon.

With the exception of a few years in Wraysbury, this is the first time that, year-round, Jan is part of the daily life of the family. He loves being surrounded by the children, who soon number seven—Tia is born in 1953 and Frank in 1955. Jan is intrigued by all the different personalities gathered around the dinner table, and takes their foibles in stride. In 1953, in a letter to Marie (at the beach with the children), he wishes her "obedient and helpful children. No, that's not possible. But that's okay. Let's just keep the bunch we have!"

In 1956, Jan is transferred to Washington, D.C., as press and cultural counselor at The Netherlands' Embassy there. The family settles into a lovely house on Massachusetts Avenue, casual enough for seven children and formal enough for frequent entertaining.

Arrival in New York. August 1956.
From left: Jan, Bernadette, Marie, Jan, and Tia, Colette and Frank, Thérèse, Liduine

In 1959, a quarter of a century after accompanying Queen Wilhelmina on her tour of partly liberated Holland, Jan proudly accompanies her granddaughter, Princess Beatrix, on a state visit to New York. The visit commemorates the 350th anniversary of New York's founding by Dutch explorer Henry Hudson.

After eight years in Washington, in 1964, Jan is promoted to the post of Consul General in San Francisco. By now, the three oldest children have left home. Thérèse and Colette have married Americans and will eventually become U.S. citizens. Jan too has married; he and his Dutch wife currently live in France.

San Francisco soon feels like home to Jan and Marie and their four youngest children. They live there until Jan's retirement in 1973. One of Jan's proudest achievements in San Francisco is the establishment of a Chair of Dutch Language and Literature at the University of California, Berkeley. The San Francisco *Chronicle* describes Jan's reluctant farewell: "When Netherlands Consul General, Jan van Houten, returns to his homeland next month he says he will be 'an unofficial emissary of San Francisco' … He has been here nine years. 'The normal tour of duty is four years, but I love San Francisco so much I asked that my time be extended.'" The article refers to Jan and Marie's seven children, and quotes Jan: "I may be an old square in many ways, but I love to hear the views of the young. Wherever we have lived, our house has always been filled with young people."

By now Bernadette and Liduine have graduated from college. Liduine marries and settles in Belgium. Bernadette spends a few more years in San Francisco. Eventually, she too moves to Holland. Here she meets her future husband.

Jan and Marie depart San Francisco in the summer of 1973 with their two youngest children, Tia and Frank. Despite their Dutch citizenship, neither Frank nor Tia has ever lived in Holland. They were toddlers when the family first sailed on the *S.S. Nieuw Amsterdam* from Rotterdam to New York. Seventeen years later, they are in college in the States. Yet both return to Holland, eventually marrying and raising their families there.

Jan and Marie return to the family's old neighborhood in The Hague. In retirement, Jan finds the peace that was missing for so many years. He has time to relax, to update his extensive stamp collection, and to play bridge with old friends and former colleagues. With Marie and visiting grandchildren, he goes for walks in nearby Park Clingendael. The grandchildren don't know that this estate was once the home of Seyss-Inquart, the notorious Nazi *Reichskommissar*. It is in part for the grand- and great-grandchildren that this book is written—that the history that shaped their parents' and grandparents' lives will not be forgotten.

On August 23, 1984, quite unexpectedly, Jan dies at home of a massive heart attack. He is 76. In his obituary, Marie lists the decorations and awards earned during those difficult war years, thereby acknowledging the many sacrifices Jan made for his country, for his family, for her, and for their children:

- Officer in the Order of Oranje Nassau of The Netherlands
- Officer in the Order of Leopold II of Belgium
- Commander in the Order of the Oak Crown of the Grand Duchy of Luxembourg
- Officer in the Order of the British Empire
- Officer in the Order of the Legion of Honour of France
- Mentioned in a *Despatch for* Distinguished Service (Great Britain)*

---

* For this British honor, *Despatch* is the correct spelling.

Marie survives Jan by 11 years. She dies at age 80 on February 8, 1995, two years after being diagnosed with lung cancer. The Mass of Christian Burial is said by Rudy Huysmans, the little boy from Jan's Eindhoven billet. Sons and grandsons carry the simple wooden coffin to the gravesite, and, hand-over-hand, gently lower it into the grave.

REFERENCES

All on-line references were checked for accuracy in October and November 2014.

1 John Keegan, *The Second World War* (New York: Penguin Books, 1990), 41.

2 Ibid., 44.

3 Ibid.

4 Ibid.

5 "The Phoney War." HistoryLearningSite.co.uk. 2011. Web. Reportedly the term ""phoney war" was coined by American senator William E. Borah. Winston Churchill used the term "twilight war" to describe this period from September 1939 to May 1940.

6 "Rationing in the United Kingdom." http://en.wikipedia.org/wiki/Ministry_of_Agriculture,_Fisheries_ and_Food. Last updated Aug. 22, 2014 .

7 John Neville, *The Blitz. London, Then and Now* (London: Hodder and Stoughton, 1990), 11.

8 Ibid., 26.

9 Louis de Jong, *Het Koninkrijk der Nederlanden in de Tweede Wereldoorlog, Londen*. Vol. 9, part 1 (The Hague: Staatsuigeverij, 1979), 1.

10　Eelco N. van Kleffens, *Juggernaut over Holland. The Dutch Foreign Minister's Personal Story of the Invasion of The Netherlands* (New York: Columbia University Press, 1941), 107.

11　Henri van der Zee. *In ballingschap. De Nederlandse Kolonie in Engeland [1940-1945]* (Amsterdam: De Bezige Bij, 2005)

12　N. David J. Barnouw, "Dutch Exiles in London" in *Europe in Exile, European Communities in Britain 1940-1945*, eds., M. Conway and J. Gotovitch (New York: Berghahn Books, 2001), 223-224.

13　Keegan, 65.

14　"Arthur Seyss-Inquart". HistoryLearningSite.co.uk. 2012. Web.

15　De Jong, *Londen*, Vol. 9, part 1, 3.

16　Marja Wagenaar, *De Rijksvoorlichtingsdienst. Geheimhouden Toedekken Openbaren: De Rol van de Rijksvoorlichtingsdienst tussen 1945 en 1994* (The Hague: SDU Uitgevers, 1997), 44.

17　Anton Speekenbrink, son of Ton Speekenbrink. E-mail communication. August 11, 2014.

18　Van der Zee, *In Ballingschap*, 180.

19　Barnouw, 234.

20　"Dossier Loe de Jong" in *De Bibiliotheekvoor Ondernemers.* http://www.bibliotheek.nl/thema/kb/kb-wetenschap/33793.dossier-loe-de-jong-(1914-2005).html

21　Barnouw, 234.

22　Anthony Saunders. *Hitler's Atlantic Wall* (London: Endeavor Press, 2014) Kindle Edition.

23　*Van der Zee,* In Ballingschap, 252.

24　Keegan, 102.

25　Martin Gilbert, *The Second World War. A Complete History* (New York, Henry Holt and Company, 1989), 62.

26　Keegan, 94.

27　Gilbert, 127.

28 Francis Keegan (Frank and Eileen Keegan's youngest son). E-mail communication, August 31, 2009.

29 Edwin Webb, John Duncan and John Walton, Blitz *over Britain* (Turnbridge Wells, Kent: Spellmont, 1990), 82-90.

30 Ibid., 42-43.

31 Mike Brown. *Put That Light Out. British Civil Defense Services at War. 1939-1945* (Stroud: Sutton Publishing, 1999), 103.

32 Webb, Duncan and Walton, 188.

33 Wagenaar, 44-45.

34 Gilbert, 306.

35 Erik Hans Bax. *Modernization and Cleavage in Dutch Society. Study of Long-Term Economic and Social Change* (Rijksuniversiteit Groningen,1988).
    http://irs.ub.rug.nl/ppn/049783513

36 De Jong, *Londen*. Vol. 9, part 1, 502-503.

37 www.windsor.gov.uk/discover-the-area/wraysbury

38 Emily Oldfield, Information Assistant, Imperial War Museum, Lambeth Road, London. E-mail communication, October 29, 2007.

39 www.scripophily.net/airlim19.html

40 www.canadianrootsuk.org/historycanadiansuk.html

41 John Keegan, 236-237.

42 Ibid., 375-377.

43 Ibid., 375.

44 De Jong, *Londen*. Volume 9, part 2, 1315.

45 Ibid., 1320-21.

46 John Hilvert. *Blue Pencil Warriors. Censorship and Propaganda in World War II.* (St. Lucia, Australia: The University of Queensland Press, Distributed in the U.S.A. by Technical Impex, 1984), 2.

47 Forrest C. Pogue. *U.S. Army in World War II. European Theater of Operations. The Supreme Command* (Washington, DC: Office of the

Chief of Military History, Department of the Navy, 1954. CMH Publication) 91. http://www.ibiblio.org/hyperwar/USA/USA-E-Supreme/USA-E-Supreme-4.html

48 Webb, Duncan and Walton, 189.

49 Van der Zee, *In Ballingschap*, 307-309.

50 W. van Leer, "Anglo-Dutch Union" in *The New Statesman and Nation*, February, 26, 1944, 136-137

51 "Ruined city." http://english.nmegen.nl/visiting/history/19001945

52 De Jong, *Londen*. Vol. 9, part 2, 1383-1386.

53 Philip Paneth, *Queen Wilhelmina, Mother of The Netherlands* (London: Alliance Press, 1944).

54 De Jong, *Het Laatste Jaar*. Vol. 10a, part 1, 163-164.

55 Gilbert, 534-536.

56 Ibid.,581.

57 Ibid.,585.

58 Margry, Karel, Operatie *Market Garden, September 1944. De Bevrijding van Eindhoven. The Liberation of Eindhoven* (Eindhoven, The Netherlands: Drukkerij Lecturis, 1992), 47.

59 Gilbert, 593.

60 Van der Zee, *The Hunger Winter. Occupied Holland 1944-4* (Lincoln, University of Nebraska Press, 1998) 29-32.

61 Under Eisenhower, SHAEF was organized into three army groups: the 6th, the 12th, and the 21st. The 21st Army Group comprises the Canadian First Army and the British Second Army—to which Jan is attached.   For administrative purposes, press censorship is part of the Publicity and Psychological Warfare Section of the appropriate group. Source: "US Army Field Censors. SHAEF" in H*istory of United States and Supreme Headquarters. A.E.F. Press Censorship in the European Theatre of Operations. 1942-1945. An after-action*

report. Reproduced by 201ˢᵗ Field Press Censorship Organization, Paramus. NJ, 1950, 58-59, and 69.

62 Pogue, 91.

63 Van den Broek, 286-287.

64 JewishGen (affiliated with the Museum of Jewish Heritage, New York, NY), "Vught (Holland)," site last updated July 1998. http:/www.jewishgen.org/ForgottenCamps/Camps/VughtEngl.html

65 Walter Cronkite was a United Press war correspondent from 1942 to 1945. Source: Albert Auster, "Cronkite, Walter, U.S. Broadcast Journalist," *The Museum of Broadcast Communications,* Chicago, Illinois. http://www.museum.tv/eotvsection.php?entrycode=cronkitewal

66 Wagenaar, 50. In an overview of the RVD, Wagenaar refers to Pelt's recommendation that Jan be transferred back to London, while he (Pelt) takes over the management of Section XI in Brussels.

67 As reported by edtvnl (Dutch educational tv channel): www.youtube.com/watch?v=d8L7XjHbFV4

68 U.S. Army Field Censors, 71.

69 Wilfried Braakhuis, "The World at War. History of WW II, 1944" Nov 10-11, 1944. http://www.euronet.nl/users/wilfried/ww2/1944.htm

70 Paul van Houten, Jan's nephew, (son of Jac and Martha van Houten). E-mail communication. September 6. 2009.

71 Gilbert, 626.

72 George R. Duncan, "Putten Atrocity" in *Massacres and Atrocities of World War II in the Countries of Belgium, France, Greece and Holland.* www.http://members.iinet.au/~gduncan/ /massacres.html

73 Van der Zee. The Hunger Winter, 60-62.

74 Gerard Rutten. *Ons Koninklijk Gezin in Bevrijd Nederland* (Wageningen: Gebr. Zomer en Keuning's Uitgeversmaatschappij, 1974), 134-135.

75 Gilbert, 666.

76 Martien Venselaar, Jan's brother-in-law. Letter to Jan, April 1, 1946.

77 Richard G. Davis. *Bombing the European Axis Powers. A historical digest of the combined power offensive, 1939-1945* (Maxwell Airforce Base, Alabama: Air University Press, 2006), 283.

78 Van der Zee, *The Hunger Winter,* 175-176.

79 Ibid., 247-257.

80 De Jong, *Het Laatste Jaar II.* Volume 10b, part 2,1331.

81 Ibid.,1341-43.

82 Ibid.,1358-1360.

83 *Afwikkelingsbureau Militair Gezag. Overzicht der werkzaamheden van het Militair Gezag Gedurende de Bijzondere Staat van Beleg, 14 September 1944 – 4 Maart, 1946.* (The Hague: Het Bureau Geschiedschrijving, 1947), bijlage VI.

84 Thea Holterhues-van Houten, Jan's niece (Jac and Martha's daughter), Spring 2008.

85 Paul van Houten, September 6, 2009.

86 Van der Zee, *The Hunger Winter,* 185-188.

87 "De Tweede Wereldoorlog en Haagse Hout" in *Historisch Den Haag.* www.historischdenhaag.nl/pagina/97/de_tweede_ wereldoorlog

88 Hans Vermeulen, *De Maasbode. De bewogen geschiedenis van 'De beste courant van Nederland'* (Zwolle, The Netherlands: Waanders, 1994), 305.

89 The Daniel Schorr referred to here is, in all likelihood, the well-known news analyst. Schorr became a foreign correspondent in 1946, after serving in U.S. Army intelligence during the war. In the post-war period he covered the reconstruction of western

Europe. Source: "National Public Radio. Daniel Schorr, Senior News Analyst." http://www.npr.org/templates/story/story. php?storyId=2101143

90 A.B.M. Brans and E. Cancrinus, *Winston Churchill Bezoekt Nederland* (Leiden: A.W. Sijthoff, 1946), 23-26.

91 *"Straatnamen" in De Tweede Wereldoorlog, 1943.* http://wittebrugpark.nl/ww2/nl-43/nl-43.htm

92 Tony Judt, *Postwar: A History of Europe since 1945* (New York: Penguin Press, 2005), 85.

ADDENDA

A. SELECT BIBLIOGRAPHY

Barnouw, N. David J. "Dutch Exiles in London" in *European Exile Communities in Britain 1940-1945*. Eds. Martin Conway and José Gotovitch. New York: Berghahn Books, 2001.

De Jong, Louis. *Het Koninkrijk der Nederlanden in de Tweede Wereld Oorlog, Londen*. Vol. 9, part 1. The Hague: Staatsuitgeverij, 1979.

———. Vol. 9, part 2. The Hague: Staatsuitgeverij, 1979.

———. *Het Laatste Jaar I*. Volume 10a, part 1. The Hague: Staatsuitgeverij, 1980.

———. Vol. 10a, part 2. The Hague: Staatsuitgeverij, 1980.

———. *Het Laatste Jaar II*. Vol. 10b, Part 1. The Hague: Staatsuitgeverij, 1981.

———. Vol. 10b, Part 2. The Hague: Staatsuitgeverij, 1982.

Gilbert, Martin. *The Second World War. A Complete History*. New York: Henry Holt and Company, 1989.

Judt, Tony. Postwar: *A History of Europe since 1945*. New York: The Penguin Press, 2005.

Keegan, John. *The Second World War*. New York, NY: Penguin Books, 2005.

Lowe, Keith. *Savage Continent. Europe in the Aftermath of World War II*. New York: St. Martin's Press, 2012.

Pogue, Forrest C. *U.S. Army in World War II. European Theater of Operations. The Supreme Command*. Washington, DC: Office of the Chief of Military History (CMH), Department of the Navy, 1954, 90. CMH Publication 7-1.http://www.ibiblio.org/hyperwar/USA/USA-E-Supreme/index.html

Van der Zee, Henri. *The Hunger Winter. Occupied Holland 1944-45*. Lincoln: University of Nebraska Press, 1998.

———. *In Ballingschap. De Nederlandse Kolonie in Engeland [1940-1945]*, Amsterdam: De Bezige Bij, 2005.

Webb, Edwin, John Duncan, and John Walton. *Blitz over Britain*. Turnbridge Wells, Kent: 1990.

B. GLOSSARY OF FOREIGN TERMS

Apéritif (French) – before-dinner or before-lunch drink.

Coletteke (Dutch) – Diminutive version of Colette.

Coûte que coûte (French) – Whatever the cost

Dag (Dutch) – Literally: day. Used as a greeting, it can mean "hello" or "goodbye."

Des bisous (French) – Little kisses.

Engeland (Dutch) – England.

Engelandvaarders (Dutch) – Literally: [sea]farers to England. In the narrow sense, the term defines those who escaped by boat from Holland to England. However, the term is also used to designate those who escaped following a perilous overland journey to neutral Portugal or Gibraltar.

Ersatz (German) – Fake or substitute, as in ersatz coffee.

Escargot (French) – Snail.

Fauteuil (Dutch and French) – Armchair.

Herrijzend (Dutch) – Rising again.

Honger (Dutch) – Hunger.

Ik ben er kapot van (Dutch expression) – It has destroyed me.

Jan (Dutch) – John; an abbreviation of Johannes.

Janneman (Dutch) – A diminutive version or nickname for Jan. It derives from the alliteration of "Jan" and "man." Literally: Jan the man.

Jantje (Dutch) - Diminutive version of Jan.

Kapitein (Dutch) – Captain.

Kerk (Dutch) – Church.

Kind (Dutch) – Child.

Kinderen, kindertjes (Dutch) – Children, little children.

Kindje (Dutch) – Literally: little child. Can also be a term of endearment.

Kindjelief (Dutch) – Dear child.

Kommandant (Dutch) – Commander.
Koninklijk (Dutch) – Royal.
Konzentrationslager (German) – Concentration Camp.
Lief, lieve (Dutch) – Dear (adjective).
Liefje (Dutch) – Dear one (noun).
Lisboa (Portuguese) – Lisbon
Londen (Dutch) – London.
Luftwaffe (German) – Air Force.
Marechaussee (Dutch) – Military police
Meisje, meiske (Dutch) –Literally: girl, little girl. Can also be a term of endearment.
Mijn (Dutch) – Mine.
Nederland (Dutch) – The Netherlands.
Nieuw (Dutch) – New.
Ontvangst (Dutch) – Reception.
Oom (Dutch) – Uncle.
Oorlog (Dutch) – War.
Opa (Dutch) – Grandfather.
Oranje (Dutch) – The color orange. The Dutch royal family descends from the House of Orange Nassau, a branch of the German House of Nassau. The color orange is therefore as much as symbol of The Netherlands as its red, white, and blue flag.
Oranje boven (Dutch) – Orange above all!
Partir c'est mourir un peu (French expression) – Literally: to leave is to die a little.
Pousse (French) – A *pousse café is* a liqueur served following after-dinner coffee.
Quel embarrass de choix (French expression) – What an embarrassment of choices.
Razzia (Dutch) – In World War II, deportation of Jews, as well as round-ups of able-bodied men for forced labor in Germany.

Regeringsbrood (Dutch) – Literally: government bread. Bread issued by the government during and after WWII.

Reichskommissar (German) – Literally: commissioner of the empire. In WWII, Hitler gave this title to governors or administrators of several occupied countries, including The Netherlands.

Schat, schatje (Dutch) – Literally: treasure, little treasure. A term of endearment.

Schatjelief (Dutch) – Literally: dear treasure. A term of endearment.

Schutzstaffel (German) – Usually abbreviated as SS. The literal meaning of *Schutzstaffel* is Protective Squadron. Initially members the SS served as Hitler's personal bodyguards. Later the squadron became a feared paramilitary Nazi organization responsible for many wartime atrocities, including the running of concentration camps. Source: *SS. World War II*. History.com

Sicherheitsdienst (German) – Security service.

Sicherheitspolizei (German) – Security police.

Tante (Dutch and French) – Aunt.

Ten paleize (Dutch) – At the palace.

Treesje, Treeske (Dutch)– diminutives of Thérèse.

Tweede wereldoorlog (Dutch) – World War II.

Une bise (French) – A kiss.

Vin rosé (French) - A rosé wine.

Vrij (Dutch)– Free.

We zijn weer vrij. (Dutch) – We are free again.

Wehrmacht (German) – Armed Forces of Germany during WWII.

Wijf, wijfje (Dutch) – Wife, little wife.

C. DUTCH ACRONYMS

ANEFO

Algemeen Nederlands Fotobureau. The Netherlands' photo service, initiated during World War II by the London-based Netherlands' press and information services.

ANEP

Algemeen Nederlands Persbureau. The Netherlands' press service in London during World War II. The acronym ANEP was used to distinguish it from the ANP, the press service in The Netherlands that was then under German control.

ANP

Algemeen Nederlands Persbureau. The Netherlands' press service. During the war it was under German control.

RPD

Regeringspersdienst. The Dutch government's press service during World War II. The forerunner of the RVD.

RVD

Rijksvoorlichtingsdienst. The Dutch government's information service during and after World War II.

D. JAN'S IMMEDIATE FAMILY IN 1945:

His Parents and Siblings

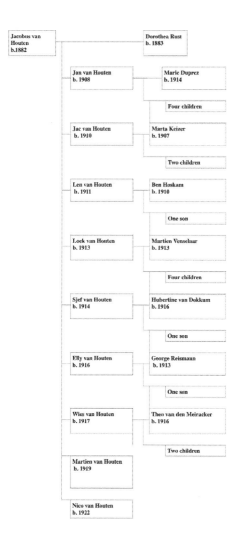

E. MARIE'S IMMEDIATE FAMILY IN 1945:

Her Parents and Siblings, her Niece and Nephew

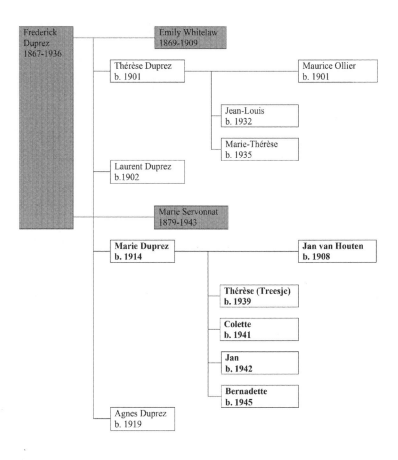

Frederick Duprez 1867-1936
Emily Whitelaw 1869-1909

Thérèse Duprez b. 1901 — Maurice Ollier b. 1901

Jean-Louis b. 1932

Marie-Thérèse b. 1935

Laurent Duprez b.1902

Marie Servonnat 1879-1943

Marie Duprez b. 1914 — Jan van Houten b. 1908

Thérèse (Treesje) b. 1939

Colette b. 1941

Jan b. 1942

Bernadette b. 1945

Agnes Duprez b. 1919

ACKNOWLEDGEMENTS

Papa's War could not have been written had my parents not kept the letters they wrote each other during and after World War II. I am forever grateful that they realized the importance of these letters and that my mother, despite some initial misgivings in the last months of her life, decided that "yes" these letters should be preserved. Nor could this book have been written without the support of my siblings: Colette, who shares with me a memory of the last war years in England and our initial post-war arrival in The Netherlands; Jan and Bernadette, who, little as they were, are an integral part of *Papa's War*; Liduine, the only sibling born in The Netherlands; Tia and Frank, the youngest two without whom our family would not be complete. For their encouragement and suggestions, I thank them.

I started out writing a small volume for family members. I cannot express sufficient thanks to the friends who, after reading an initial draft of *Papa's War*, encouraged me to write for a broader audience: Barbara Stout, Liz Dyson, Patricia Fagen, Cissie Coy, and Linda Harteker. Linda's patience and forbearance in listening to my ideas about the book's many iterations were truly inspiring. It is she who introduced me to my wonderful editor, Heather Dittbrenner. Heather's editorial insight, keen eye, attention to detail, and focused questions have ensured consistency in style, tone and content. A special shout-out to my granddaughters Johanna and Emma for double-checking last minute details.

I am grateful for the assistance provided by the librarians at the Cleveland Park Library in Washington, D.C. in locating books, studies, and after-action reports on the exiled Dutch government, and the post-war role of the Dutch and allied military. I was very fortunate as well to get historical input from two historians, one American, the other Dutch: my good friend Mary Jane Hamilton, and a cousin, Frans van Eekelen. *Papa's War* would not be the same without the family photos reformatted by my son Peter Belanger, and the text-relevant map of The Netherlands provided by my daughter-in-law Amy Gregg.

Cousins Thea Holterhues and her brother Paul van Houten shared painful memories of a childhood interrupted by war. Other cousins, Conny van Houten, Jan Hoskam, Marijke van Eekelen and Hans Reismann, helped search for photos taken by family members immediately after the bombing of Rotterdam. Yet another cousin, Jack Venselaar, provided invaluable feedback on an early draft; his sisters Wies Tuinder and Dorothé Tempelman sent me a copy of a letter written by their father a year after liberation. To all a resounding thank you.

And last but certainly not least, I thank my awesome children: Edward, Johannes, Suzanne, Peter and Helena. They are my strongest supporters: their love and encouragement never cease to amaze.

Made in the USA
Charleston, SC
04 May 2015